Martin Bosley Cooks.

Photographs by Jane Ussher

Mart

Bosl

Cook

RANDOM HOUSE
NEW ZEALAND

To Julia and Isabella, who have never stopped believing, allow me my passion, eat the food I cook for them, and have never told me to get a real job.

A catalogue record for this book is available from the National Library of New Zealand

A Random House Book
published by
Random House New Zealand
18 Poland Road, Glenfield,
Auckland, New Zealand

Random House International
Random House
20 Vauxhall Bridge Road
London, SW1V 2SA
United Kingdom

Random House Australia Pty Ltd
Level 3, 100 Pacific Highway
North Sydney 2060, Australia

Random House South Africa Pty Ltd
Isle of Houghton
Corner Boundary Road and Carse O'Gowrie
Houghton 2198, South Africa

Random House Publishers India Private Ltd
301 World Trade Tower, Hotel
Intercontinental Grand Complex
Barakhamba Lane, New Delhi 110 001, India

ISBN 978 1 86979 035 6

First published 2008

Design: Seven.co.nz
Printed in China by South China
Printing Co. Ltd.

Bread 16/
Soup 30/
Salad 50/
Light Meals 78/
Mains 136/
Desserts & Baking 192/

Butters & Sauces 254/
Drinks 268/
Liquid Assets 278/

Index 285.

Martin Bosley Cooks.

Yes, well, it's what I do. For me the kitchen is at the centre of my world. It is where everything takes place, both at work and at home. Everybody ends up there; it's where we meet, talk, discuss and laugh, surrounded by good food and usually good wine. I am a cook and the kitchen is where I am most comfortable, with a tea towel over my shoulder, a glass of wine in hand. Cooking is what I have always done, and I can't imagine doing anything else. It brings me such great satisfaction and peace of mind. I adore food, it is no secret, and I adore it in all its ways, from the simplest to the most creative.

The most frequent question I am asked is whether I cook at home, and if so, what is it that I eat. The answer is that, yes, I do cook at home, and what I cook is the sort of food that's in this book — because it's easy to achieve. I, too, lead a busy life, have a family, and find myself time poor. In fact my work hours are possibly worse than most, so I know what it's like to try to find the time to spend in the kitchen at home.

But the philosophies about cooking and eating that I use in my restaurant are the same for my personal cooking life: I eat what is in season, I eat what is fresh, and, as much as I can, I eat what is locally produced. I know it's not always convenient to do this, but the food decisions we make are one of the few freedoms of choice we have left, so it's worth the effort, I think. Stop at roadside stalls, support your local butcher or greengrocer, find a farmers' market. Even if you are only able to shop like this on just one day of the week, you will enjoy the rewards from not only the amazing produce but also from the relationships you build. Food, and eating, is a social event, so embrace it.

Good food needs good ingredients, and eating seasonally is not a new trend, nor is it just about reducing food miles. Fundamentally, it is about what is healthy for our bodies and minds. It's about having respect for nature and all that it provides. Food tastes better when eaten in season, and so much of what I cook stems from just looking at produce, and taking my inspiration from it. I still marvel at the flawless perfection of an aubergine, at the textures of spankingly fresh fish, and my pulse rate quickens at the smell of fresh basil or lemon verbena. My year rolls across ingredients, each season bringing something new to look forward to.

When I began writing for the *Listener*, I was conscious of not wanting to make the food too 'restauranty', complicated and unattainable. The idea was for each column to feature recipes that would fit the concept of 'feel good to fancy'. I wanted to write about the sort of food that I cook at home, for family and friends, and to look at ingredients individually. The occasional restaurant dish does sneak in, but only because I genuinely believe it is possible to replicate it at home. I wanted to look at the sorts of ingredients we're capable of using every day, the sorts of ingredients that are accessible to us all. For example, I use store-bought chicken stock at home and people always seem surprised when I tell them this. I know why: they think I handcraft my own, lovingly skimming the stock through the small hours of the morning as it gently cooks over the flame from a lit match. However, I want convenience just as much as the next person does.

Most of all, through the column I wanted to encourage people to get into their kitchens and acquaint themselves with their stoves. My home kitchen is like anyone else's — it's not full of wonderful, fancy gadgets, there are no ice-cream machines lurking in the corner, and no shiny rack of highly polished copper pans hangs from the ceiling. Instead it is purely functional, full of natural light, with the stove, a Kenwood mixer I have had since Adam was a lad, and an ancient butcher's block bought at auction 20-plus years ago taking centre stage. When I was younger I had a knife-roll full of tools, 15 different knives and a selection of corers, ballers and scoops. The more I cook, the fewer tools I need; I find myself using the same knife for everything and I tend not to make pearl-sized balls out of my vegetables at home! What the column was not to be was yet another one that told you how to make gravy, how to boil an egg or roast a chicken; there are enough food magazines available already that can tell you how to do that.

The recipes are not my artistic and creative food statement to the world. Instead the column is about the simple food that stems from my love of cooking, of eating and of encouraging others to do the same. The recipes, like all good recipes, are driven by taste rather than creativity and presentation. Those both come into it later, naturally, but I want others to enjoy that feeling of comfort and generosity that comes from preparing good food for others. There is no greater pleasure.

The recipes are largely pieced together from scraps of paper that I write ideas down on, or from the conversations I have with my team of talented cooks, my suppliers, restaurant guests, family and friends. Some of the recipes were created years ago, at previous restaurants I have had. The chocolate terrine was developed 20 years ago and has never been off any of my menus, and it still continues to delight.

Recognising that what is available at the beginning of a season is usually not available at the end of it, this book is organised instead into meal categories as opposed to seasonal chapters. Ideally, use this book as a reference guide, or a source of inspiration, for the ingredients available to you. The recipes are simply a guideline because weights, measures and cooking times may vary, so apply yourself to learning to recognise when things look done. Most of all, and probably the best advice that I can give, is to relax. It's only food, not rocket science.

BUTTERCUPS
·70¢ each
2 for $1·30
PUMPKINS
1·60¢ each
2 for $3·00

Bread.

With so many commercial breads being fluffy yet lifeless, it is tremendously satisfying to experience the bliss of a slice of freshly baked homemade bread. Even better if you make it yourself — it's easier to do than most people realise. I think the time it takes puts people off, but really the dough does all the work. After assembling ingredients, you only spend about 30 minutes making the bread; the rest is leaving it to prove.

I prefer to use fresh yeast, but you can substitute dried granules, using half the quantity of dried yeast to fresh. One tablespoon of dried yeast leavens one kilogram of flour, but always dissolve it in water first. Fresh yeast can be added directly to the flour.

This Section

Brioche   **18**

Fruit Bread   **20**

Simple Bread Rolls   **23**

Brioche —

Buttery, soft and delicate, with a tender crumb — that's brioche. Served for breakfast or brunch, it revives the most jaded tastebuds. It's like a warm hug. Serve it hot with preserves, or topped with something more savoury.

Ingredients / Makes 2 loaves

30g fresh yeast
500ml warm milk
60g sugar
1 tsp salt
500g flour
5 eggs
150g unsalted butter, softened
1 egg, beaten, to glaze the bread

Method

Heat the oven to 200°C. Into a mixer bowl put the yeast, warm milk, sugar and salt. Beat lightly on a low speed with the dough hook. Add the flour and eggs, and knead for about 10 minutes until smooth and elastic. Add the softened butter a little at a time. Once all the butter is added, mix for a further 15 minutes. Cover the bowl with a wet tea towel, and leave for two hours to double in volume. Turn the dough onto a floured bench and knock the air out of it with your fingertips, flip and repeat. Shape into a large ball and divide it in two. Place each portion into greased and floured bread tins. Brush the tops with the beaten egg. Place the dough in a warm place to prove again for about 20 minutes. Snip the tops with scissors. Bake for 45 minutes, then remove from the tins immediately and cool on a wire rack.

Fruit Bread —

This is fabulous served with cheese and fresh dates, and drizzled with honey.

Ingredients / Makes 8–10 buns or 2 loaves

100g dried figs	
60g pitted prunes	
125g raisins	
½ cup boiling water	
¼ cup honey	
1 tsp grated lemon zest	
2 tsp fresh yeast	
1 tsp sugar	
300ml water	
1 tsp salt	
1 egg	
600g flour	
2 tsp cinnamon	
1 egg, beaten	

Method

Roughly chop the figs and prunes and add the raisins. Mix the boiling water with the honey and lemon zest and pour it over the fruit. Set aside. Into a mixer bowl put the yeast, sugar, water and salt. Add the egg and flour and, using the dough hook on low speed for about 15 minutes, mix to form a smooth dough. Cover the bowl with a damp tea towel to prove the dough for one hour. Drain the fruit, reserving the liquid. Stir the cinnamon into the fruit and knead it into the dough. Tip the dough onto a floured bench, shape it into loaves, and place on a greased and floured baking tray. Place somewhere warm to prove the dough again for 15–20 minutes. Mix a little leftover syrup with the beaten egg and brush it on top of the loaves. Bake for 15 minutes in an oven preheated to 200°C. Remove the bread from the oven, brush again with the syrup, lower the temperature to 180°C and return to the oven for a further 25 minutes. Transfer to a wire cooling rack.

Simple Bread Rolls —

This recipe will produce charmingly seductive and soft rolls.

Ingredients / Makes 8–10 rolls or 2 loaves

500ml water
30g fresh or 15g dried yeast
900g flour
60g sugar
30g salt

Method

Preheat the oven to 200°C with a shallow dish of water in the bottom — the steam helps to produce a nice crust. If using dried yeast, mix the water and yeast together in a bowl and place in a warm place for 15–20 minutes. Add fresh yeast to the flour mix. In a separate bowl mix the flour, sugar and salt. Combine the two sets of ingredients together in a mixer bowl and, using the dough hook, mix on low speed until the dough is smooth and starts to leave the sides of the bowl. It will look quite wet. Place in a warm place to prove and double in volume for about two hours. Turn the dough onto a floured bench and knock back gently using the palms of your hands. Divide the mixture into 100-grams balls. Using a cupped hand, form into smooth rolls. Place onto a greased tray and cover with cling film. Leave the tray in a warm place to prove the dough again for 20–30 minutes. Dust the tops of the rolls with flour and cut the top of each with a sharp knife. Bake for 15–20 minutes. When done, the bottoms should sound hollow when tapped. Remove the tray from the oven and transfer rolls to a wire cooling rack.

Soup.

Soup is one of those dishes I rarely order in restaurants. It is easy to make, but just as easy to get wrong and, more often than not, I have been disappointed.

In the thick of winter I have eagerly ordered pumpkin soup, expecting something perfumed and silky, only to be served a bowl of thick, lumpy, watery-tasting, bright-orange sludge. And I also remember a particularly bad French onion soup, with only a token sprinkling of what should have been an intoxicating amount of deeply caramelised brown onions, and a garnish of two-day-old, greasy-cheese-covered dried bread.

For me, one of life's simple pleasures is making soup. Soups define a nation's culture. Good soup brings comfort and smiles. It's the kindest course in a three-course meal or may be served as dinner by itself. For a small amount of effort, you can be rewarded with delicious and fragrant broths; bisques thickened with shellfish; or rich and velvety soups thickened with eggs and cream. Simplest of all, though, are the puréed soups, which can provide indulgent and astonishingly good flavours.

This Section

Pea and Smoked Ham Soup
with Mushrooms and Raisins   **33**

Asparagus Soup with
Goat's Curd   **34**

Jerusalem Artichoke
and Apple Soup   **36**

Bourride Soup   **39**

Easy Winter Seafood
Chowder with Crumbled
Water Crackers   **40**

Stephen's Paua Soup
with Fried Capers   **43**

Straciatella   **44**

Pea and Smoked Ham Soup with Mushrooms and Raisins —

This pea and ham soup uses frozen peas rather than split-dried. Most restaurants use frozen peas as the flavour is better, the soup has a more seductive texture and the emerald-green colour is extremely elegant. It's perfect on a chilly evening.

Ingredients / Serves 6

Stock
Makes 2.5 litres

2 tbsp unsalted butter
1 cup chopped onions
1 small leek, white part only, chopped
2 stalks celery, chopped
1 bay leaf
1 pinch fresh thyme leaves
1 tsp black peppercorns
2 cloves garlic, chopped
200ml white wine
1 smoked ham hock, approximately 1kg
3 rashers bacon, chopped
4 litres water

Soup

400g peas (if using frozen peas, thaw first)
1 litre ham stock, hot
optional: 1 tbsp lemon-infused olive oil
salt and freshly ground black pepper
2 tbsp unsalted butter
1 cup finely sliced button mushrooms
2 tbsp diced smoked ham
1 tbsp raisins, soaked in 2 tbsp of hot ham stock

Method

To make the stock, melt the butter in a heavy-based saucepan or stockpot over a medium heat. Add the vegetables, herbs, peppercorns and garlic, and cook until they are golden and slightly softened. Add the wine and simmer until it has reduced by half. Add the hock, bacon and water to the pot. Bring it to a gentle simmer and cook for 1½ hours. Remove the hock and set aside. Strain the stock, discard the vegetables and return the liquid to the pot. Bring it back to the boil and simmer until it has reduced by one-third. This will make more than you need, so freeze the rest. Remove the meat from the hock and dice.

To make the soup, place the peas in a large bowl and pour over the stock. Then place the peas and stock into a liquidiser or blender (you may need to do this in batches) and purée until velvety smooth. Add the olive oil, if using, and season with salt and pepper. Return the soup to a pot and keep it warm. If you want to preserve the emerald-green colour, do not heat for too long. (If you want to make the soup ahead and still preserve the colour, chill it immediately after blending.) In a frying pan, melt the butter then gently sauté the mushrooms for a few minutes. Add the smoked ham and raisins and warm through. Season lightly with salt and freshly ground black pepper.

To Serve

Pour the soup into bowls and place a teaspoon of the mushroom, ham and raisin mixture in the centre of each bowl.

Asparagus Soup with Goat's Curd —

To make truly exquisite asparagus soup you need to use fresh whole spears, not just the woody ends or peelings.

Ingredients / Serves 6

100g unsalted butter
6 shallots, peeled and chopped
1 bunch spinach, washed and trimmed
1 potato, peeled and chopped
150ml white wine
600ml chicken stock or water
450g asparagus, trimmed and peeled
300ml cream
salt and freshly ground black pepper
4 tbsp Summerlee goat's curd, crème fraîche or sour cream
2 tbsp extra virgin olive oil for serving

Method

Melt the butter and fry the shallots for about five minutes until soft but not coloured. Add the spinach, potato, wine and stock and cook for 15 minutes. Add the asparagus and cook for five minutes. Purée the soup in a liquidiser and then pour it through a fine sieve. Add the cream and season with salt and black pepper.

To Serve

Pour into bowls and add a spoonful of goat's curd to each one. Sprinkle with olive oil. This soup may be served hot or cold.

Jerusalem Artichoke and Apple Soup —

One of the most elegant of soups. To prevent the artichokes from discolouring, peel them and plunge them into a bowl of cold water with a little lemon juice in it.

Ingredients / Serves 6

1 tbsp unsalted butter
1 cup chopped onion
2 stalks celery, chopped
1 small leek, white part only, chopped
1 bay leaf
1 tsp black peppercorns
2 apples, peeled, cored and chopped
1 cup cider or dry white wine
1kg Jerusalem artichokes, peeled and chopped
500ml chicken stock
600ml cream
salt to taste
chopped chives or croutons to garnish

Method

In a heavy-based saucepan, melt the butter and add the onion, celery, leek, bay leaf, peppercorns and apple. Cook over a low heat until soft and without colour. Add the cider or wine and continue cooking until the liquid has reduced by half. Add the artichokes cream and stock, and bring to a gentle simmer. Cook for 30–40 minutes until the artichokes are tender. Remove the bay leaf and purée the soup in a liquidiser or blender until velvety smooth.

To Serve

Season lightly with salt and garnish with chives or croutons.

Bourride Soup —

In terms of lightness and simplicity, the bourride fish soup recipe marked a turning point in my cookery, and I still refer to it now when I think my food might be too complicated. Bourride is a classic Mediterranean fish soup-stew in the style of bouillabaisse, but without the saffron and the dozen varieties of fish that are normally required. Just use any available firm-fleshed white fish, such as groper or monkfish. A long list of ingredients can be offputting, but once they're assembled, this soup is easy to make. I usually cook my vegetables a couple of days ahead, so all that's required is to reheat them with the fish and thicken the soup.

Ingredients / Serves 4

4 thick slices of baguette
4 tbsp olive oil
1 leek, white part only, thinly sliced
1 onion, thinly sliced
1 carrot, thinly sliced
2 cloves garlic, sliced
2 tbsp coarsely chopped fresh parsley, fennel and thyme
2–3 strips orange peel
1 bay leaf
500g assorted fish, cut into 3-cm cubes
300ml water
200ml vermouth
5 egg yolks
100ml cream
2 tsp mayonnaise or aïoli
sea salt and freshly ground black pepper

Method

Heat the oven to 180°C. Brush the baguette slices using two tablespoons of the olive oil. Bake the bread until golden brown and crusty — about seven minutes. Place a piece of baked baguette in the bottom of four individual bowls. In a deep pot heat the remaining olive oil and add the leek, onion, carrot, garlic, herbs, peel and bay leaf. Sauté until the vegetables become soft, shiny and aromatic.

Arrange the pieces of fish over the vegetables. Pour the water and vermouth over the top and bring to a lazy simmer. Cook for 10 minutes. Using a slotted spoon, divide the fish among the four bowls. Remove the pot from the heat.

Whisk the egg yolks with the cream and mayonnaise and pour them into the still-hot liquid. Return the pot to a low heat and whisk until the mixture thickens. Do not boil or you will scramble the eggs. Season with salt and pepper.

To Serve

Pour generous ladles of vegetables and broth over the fish. Serve immediately.

Easy Winter Seafood Chowder with Crumbled Water Crackers —

This a great winter's weekend soup that just seems to taste better if you are at the seaside when eating it.

Ingredients / Serves 6

80g unsalted butter

1 medium onion, finely chopped

1 litre milk

500ml cream

1 tsp fresh thyme leaves

500g peeled potatoes, diced

1kg white-fleshed fish, cut into 3-cm cubes or

1 cup of steamed cockle meat or 2 dozen oysters

sea salt and freshly ground black pepper

100g bacon, diced and precooked
(I do this in the microwave)

2 tbsp chopped parsley and water-cracker crumbs to garnish

Method

Melt the butter in a large saucepan or stockpot and sauté the onion for about two to three minutes until translucent and without colour. Add the milk and cream and simmer for 20 minutes. Dice the thyme leaves and add to the chowder. Add the potatoes and simmer until tender. Add the seafood and simmer until just cooked through. Season to taste with salt and pepper, then add the bacon.

To Serve

Sprinkle the chowder with parsley and crumbled water crackers if desired.

Stephen's Paua Soup with Fried Capers —

Developed by Stephen Mahoney, my head chef, the secret to this soup, and its incredible depth of flavour and texture, comes from the initial braising of the paua, which takes two hours. It may seem a long time to wait for a bowl of soup but trust me it is more than worth it.

Ingredients / Serves 6

Stock

1 onion, chopped
3 sticks of celery, chopped
2 bay leaves
4 large paua, cleaned and scrubbed
500ml chicken stock

Soup

50g unsalted butter
½ onion, chopped
1 stick of celery, chopped
½ leek, white part only, chopped
cooked paua, chopped
1 bay leaf
100ml dry vermouth
100ml paua stock
400ml milk
400ml cream
salt and freshly ground black pepper
chopped chives for serving

Fried Capers

1 tbsp olive oil
2 tbsp capers, rinsed

Method

First you need to braise the paua, and this takes some time. Preheat the oven to 180°C. Place the onion, celery, bay leaves and the cleaned paua into a deep ovenproof pot and pour over the chicken stock. Cover with a piece of greaseproof paper and then with some tinfoil. Bring the liquid to a simmer on top of the stove and then place the pot in the oven. Cook for two hours and then remove the pot from the oven. Strain and reserve the liquid, measuring out 100ml and set it to one side, but discard the vegetables. Cool the paua until you are able to handle them and slice them into ½-centimetre thick pieces. Set to one side.

In a deep saucepan melt the butter and stir in the onion, celery and leek, and cook until they begin to soften. Then add the paua and bay leaf and lower the heat. Pour in the vermouth and cook for two minutes and then pour in the paua stock and cook for another two minutes. Add the milk and cream and bring the soup to the boil, then turn down the heat so that the soup gently simmers for 20 minutes. Remove the bay leaf and transfer the contents of the pot to a blender and purée until smooth and season.

To fry the capers, heat a frying pan and add the oil. Once it is hot, quickly sauté the capers until they pop open and then remove them to a paper towel to drain.

To Serve
Sprinkle the soup with the capers and chopped chives.

Straciatella —

This is a thin broth enriched with Parmesan and eggs.

Ingredients / Serves 4

4 eggs

4 tbsp grated Parmesan cheese

pinch of nutmeg

800ml chicken stock

Method

Break the eggs into a bowl and beat lightly with a fork. Add the cheese and nutmeg and 200ml of the stock. Put the remaining stock in a pot over a low heat and bring to a simmer, then remove from the heat. Pour in the egg mixture, whisking continuously. Place the soup back over the heat and allow it to come back to a gentle simmer. Threads of egg mixture should be broken up through the stock. Serve immediately.

Salad.

The key to a good salad is not letting great ingredients become confused or overwhelmed by too many flavours. The following recipes have been designed to be used as a toolbox of flavours and accompaniments and to stimulate your own ideas. The salads can be served on their own or with the other dishes. My favourite herbs — basil, tarragon, chervil, chives — are in abundance in summer. They make a meal fit for a king when combined in a salad with locally grown tomatoes and served with grilled fish.

Most of all, relax and allow the rhythm of the seasons to suggest what you cook. Happy eating.

This Section

Asparagus Salad with
Soft-boiled-egg Dressing **53**

Salad of Broad Beans,
Pecorino Cheese and Mint **54**

Scallop Caesar Salad with
Horseradish Vinaigrette **57**

White Bean Salad,
Young Fennel and
Gruyère Cheese **58**

Citrus-cured Salmon,
Radish, Fennel and
Cucumber Salad **61**

Italian-style Bread
and Tomato Salad **63**

Plum and Goat's Cheese
Salad with Ginger Syrup **64**

Roasted Sweet Potato,
Pea and Ham Salad with
Lemon Mayonnaise **67**

Salad of Jerusalem Artichokes,
Almonds and Watermelon with
Honeyed Olive Oil Dressing **68**

Salad of Scarlet Runner Beans
with Tomatoes, Almonds and
Sweet Onion Vinaigrette **72**

Asparagus Salad with
Soft-boiled-egg Dressing —

Asparagus is as much about taste as it is about texture, so I prefer to use the plumper-stemmed asparagus rather than those with pencil-thin stems. Thickness has no bearing on tenderness because if the asparagus is fresh it will also be tender. To test for this, snap the spear in half with your fingers: if it's fresh, it snaps easily. To keep them that way, put the spears cut-side down in a container with a couple of centimetres of water and refrigerate. Before cooking, I snap off the woody ends then use a vegetable peeler to peel the bottom three centimetres. It may seem extreme, but it is worth the extra effort.

This mayonnaise-based recipe is a variation on the classic pairing of asparagus served with a poached egg. With its selection of fresh herbs, the dressing is the perfect accompaniment to asparagus. Serve either as a simple entrée or as a dip on a platter so that guests can dip the emerald-green spears into it. The dressing may also be used with salad leaves or as a sandwich filling.

Ingredients / Serves 6–8

4 egg yolks

1 tbsp grain mustard

2 tbsp white wine vinegar

2 tbsp chopped tarragon

2 tbsp chopped chives

2 tbsp chopped chervil

2 tbsp chopped parsley

500ml olive oil

5 eggs, soft boiled for 4 minutes, cooled and peeled

juice of 2 lemons

1 tbsp sugar

salt and freshly ground black pepper

30 plump spears of asparagus, trimmed and peeled

lemon juice to serve

sea salt and pepper to serve

Method

In a food processor combine the yolks, mustard, vinegar and herbs. Blend for three minutes. With the processor still running, slowly add the oil, a few drops to begin with, gradually increasing to a thin, steady stream. This will make a rich mayonnaise. Roughly chop the soft-boiled eggs and fold through the mayonnaise. Add the juice from one lemon, then the sugar and season with salt and pepper. Pour the dressing into a jar and refrigerate. It will keep in the refrigerator for 10 days. Bring a large pot of salted water to a rolling boil and add the asparagus. Cook for three to four minutes, drain and wrap in a wet tea towel until ready to serve.

To Serve

Place the asparagus on a serving platter, squeeze over a little lemon juice, season with sea salt and black pepper and serve with the dressing on the side.

Salad of Broad Beans, Pecorino Cheese and Mint —

You can use Parmesan instead for this delightfully simple salad, if you don't enjoy the earthy punchiness of sheep's milk cheese.

Ingredients / Serves 4

1kg broad beans, in their pods

½ preserved lemon (available from delis), rinsed and finely chopped

100g pecorino, thinly sliced

salt and freshly ground black pepper

8 mint leaves, finely sliced

juice of 1 lemon

olive oil to taste

Method

Shell the beans and plunge them into boiling water for six minutes. Run them under cold water, then remove the skins. This is called double-podding. (If the beans are young and tender, you will not need to do this.) You should end up with one cup of beans.

To Serve

Combine with the remaining ingredients and serve.

Scallop Caesar Salad with Horseradish Vinaigrette —

Freshly shucked scallops served raw with only the juice of a lemon to garnish are hard to beat. These rich, delicate morsels wrap themselves around the tongue to give a burst of flavour on the palate.

If you must cook scallops, these simple tips will help you get perfect results every time:

+ Oil the scallops but not the pan. In a separate bowl, pour melted unsalted butter over the scallops. Just enough butter will stick to prevent them from stewing in their own juices and turning tough and rubbery when cooked.
+ Use an extremely hot pan. You want the scallops to sear quickly and caramelise to form a golden crust.
+ To stop the scallops 'spitting' while cooking, pierce the orange coral of the roe and the white muscle using the tip of a sharp knife.
+ Avoid using cheese-based sauces — they are too heavy and strong for this mollusc's delicate flavour.

The scallop salad is a variation on the classic Caesar. Purists argue that classics shouldn't be messed with, but I think that these flavours and textures work well together.

Ingredients / Serves 4

Scallop Caesar

½ baguette, cut into 1-cm cubes

olive oil

8 rashers streaky bacon

1 cos lettuce

2 tbsp unsalted butter or olive oil

24 whole scallops

sea salt and freshly ground black pepper

juice of 1 lemon

4 tbsp horseradish vinaigrette

4 tbsp shaved Parmesan cheese to garnish

2 tbsp finely chopped chives to garnish

Horseradish Vinaigrette

3 tbsp olive oil

2 tbsp white wine vinegar

1 tsp horseradish cream

sea salt and freshly ground black pepper

Method

To make the salad, preheat the oven to 180°C. Toss the bread cubes in enough olive oil to coat and place them on a baking tray. Bake for five minutes or until golden brown. Place the bacon on a baking tray and bake until crisp, then finely slice the rashers into matchsticks. Trim the lettuce, discarding the tough exterior leaves. Roughly chop the mid-layer leaves, keeping the tender inner leaves whole. Heat a frying pan over a high heat. Melt the unsalted butter in the microwave and pour it over the scallops in a separate bowl. Alternatively, use olive oil. Add the scallops to the hot pan, turning once when golden brown. Remove from the pan and season lightly with salt, pepper and a squeeze of lemon juice.

To make the vinaigrette, whisk the ingredients until combined. It will keep in the refrigerator for at least two weeks.

To Serve

Toss the lettuce with the croutons, bacon and scallops. Drizzle with horseradish vinaigrette and scatter over the Parmesan and chives.

White Bean Salad, Young Fennel and Gruyère Cheese —

This salad works well with any grilled seafood, but especially with barbecued prawns.

Ingredients / Serves 4

440g can white beans

2 tomatoes, deseeded and cut into 1-cm dice, or sun-dried tomatoes, chopped

½ cup chicken stock

2 tbsp olive oil

juice of 1 lemon

2 tbsp chopped parsley

1 fennel bulb

½ lebanese cucumber, deseeded and diced

1 bunch spring onions, sliced

120g Gruyère cheese

salt and freshly ground black pepper

Method

Rinse the beans under cold running water and drain in a sieve. Mix with the tomato. Whisk together the stock, oil, lemon juice and parsley and set aside. Trim the tops and base off the fennel. Thinly slice the fennel on the diagonal and mix into the beans with the cucumber and spring onions. Thinly slice the cheese, stir gently through the beans and add the dressing. Season with salt and pepper.

Citrus-cured Salmon, Radish, Fennel and Cucumber Salad —

The salmon is a variation on the classic gravlax. Served with the radish salad, it's refreshing, simple and natural. Eat any leftover salmon slices on some toasted wholemeal bread as a quick snack.

Ingredients / Serves 4

Citrus-cured Salmon

zest of 1 lemon
zest of 1 lime
zest of 1 orange
4 tbsp sugar
4 tbsp salt
30ml vodka
450g fillet of salmon, skinned and boned

Radish, Fennel and Cucumber Salad

2 medium fennel bulbs, washed, trimmed and thinly sliced
4 radishes, washed and thinly sliced
1 small cucumber, deseeded and thinly sliced
salt and freshly ground black pepper
juice of 1 lemon
3 tbsp olive oil

Method

To cure the salmon, combine the citrus zests to form a smooth paste. Mix the sugar and salt together in a separate container. Sprinkle half the sugar and salt into a deep dish. Rub the vodka into one side of the salmon and spread with half the zest mixture. Place the salmon zest-side down on the sugar and salt. Sprinkle the remaining sugar and salt on the upper side and rub in the remaining zest. Cover with cling film and refrigerate for 12 hours before turning the salmon over and returning it to the refrigerator for a further 12 hours. Remove the salmon from the marinade and brush clean. Pat it dry with absorbent paper, and slice into three-millimetre thin pieces.

To make the salad, put the fennel, radishes and cucumber in a small bowl. Season with salt and pepper and add the lemon juice and olive oil. Mix thoroughly and leave for five minutes before serving alongside the sliced salmon.

Italian-style Bread and Tomato Salad —

This salad is a variation on the Italian panzanella. You need great bread and tomatoes bursting with ripeness for the best flavour — the quality of the ingredients will shine through. I remove the crusts before making the salad, but this is not essential.

Ingredients / Serves 4

½ stale baguette

8 leaves basil

4 tomatoes, deseeded and cut into cubes

1 red onion, finely sliced

½ telegraph cucumber, peeled and diced

2 cloves garlic, chopped

1 tbsp chopped parsley

2 tsp red wine or sherry vinegar

4 tbsp olive oil

salt and freshly ground black pepper

2 hard-boiled eggs, quartered, to garnish

Method

Dip the bread briefly into cold water — it should be damp, not soggy — then tear it into pieces. Add the basil, tomatoes, onion, cucumber, garlic and parsley. Sprinkle with the vinegar and olive oil and toss well. Adjust the seasoning. Let the salad sit for 30 minutes, then garnish with the eggs and serve immediately.

Plum and Goat's Cheese Salad with Ginger Syrup —

As long as the plums are ripe, it doesn't matter what variety you use for this recipe.

Ingredients / Serves 4

Ginger Syrup
Makes 1 cup

1 cup water	
½ cup sugar	
3-cm piece of root ginger, peeled and chopped	

Salad

4 ripe plums, halved, destoned and quartered	
240g soft goat's cheese	
freshly ground black pepper	
3 tbsp walnut oil	
1 tbsp cider vinegar	
1 tsp sugar	
baby lettuce leaves	
sea salt	

Method

First, make the syrup by bringing the water and sugar to the boil in a saucepan. Reduce the heat and simmer for two minutes. Add the ginger and continue to simmer for 15 minutes. Remove from the heat and strain, then let the syrup cool.

To make the salad, first toss the plum pieces in a tablespoon of the syrup. Crumble the cheese into a bowl and season with pepper. Mix the oil, vinegar and sugar to make a dressing. Lightly toss the lettuce leaves in the dressing and season with salt.

To Serve

Place the plums and cheese on individual plates and drizzle a little extra syrup around them. Arrange the leaves over the cheese and plums.

Roasted Sweet Potato, Pea and Ham Salad with Lemon Mayonnaise —

This a great lunch to make when you just want to throw a handful of things together and be eating in 30-or-so minutes. The warm sweet potato is a pleasant contrast to the cold ham.

Ingredients / Serves 6

1kg sweet potatoes, washed

olive oil

salt and freshly ground black pepper

1 cup fresh peas, shelled and cooked

180g sliced leg ham

8 mint leaves, finely sliced

½ cup lemon mayonnaise

Lemon Mayonnaise
Makes 2 cups

3 egg yolks

½ tsp Dijon mustard

a pinch of salt

juice of 1 lemon

300ml grapeseed oil

freshly ground black pepper

Method

Preheat the oven to 180°C. To prepare the salad cut the sweet potatoes into large chunks and toss lightly in oil, salt and pepper. Bake in the oven for 30 minutes or until tender. Transfer the sweet potato to a bowl and add the peas and ham. Stir in the mint and mayonnaise.

To make the lemon mayonnaise, blend the egg yolks, mustard, salt and lemon juice in a food processor until smooth. With the motor running, slowly add the oil, a few drops to begin with, gradually increasing to a thin, steady stream. When all the oil is added, taste for acidity and add more lemon juice if necessary. Season lightly with pepper. It will keep in the refrigerator for up to 10 days.

Salad of Jerusalem Artichokes, Almonds and Watermelon with Honeyed Olive Oil Dressing —

The Jerusalem artichoke has a rather sad reputation for inducing bouts of flatulence, but please do not let that dissuade you from making this delicious salad. I paired it with the watermelon because of its similar texture when eaten raw, and added the almonds for their flavour and crunch. It is a delightful entrée that looks a bit flash, but is full of wintery crispness.

Ingredients / Serves 4

3 tbsp red wine vinegar
2 tbsp honey
150ml olive oil
salt and freshly ground black pepper
500g Jerusalem artichokes, scrubbed
½ cup sliced almonds, lightly toasted
4 basil leaves, torn
1 small watermelon

Method

To make the dressing, combine the red wine vinegar with the honey in a small bowl and whisk. Add the olive oil and blend together, then season. Thinly slice the artichokes lengthways, using a sharp knife or a mandolin slicer. Place into a small bowl and lightly toss through the dressing, almonds and basil. Cut the watermelon flesh into three-centimetre-thick fingers, discarding as many seeds as is reasonably possible.

To Serve

Put a piece of watermelon on an individual plate and top with a small handful of the artichokes. Spoon over any extra dressing.

Salad of Scarlet Runner Beans with Tomatoes, Almonds and Sweet Onion Vinaigrette —

You'll rarely find scarlet runners in supermarkets, which is a shame. I get my supply from my mother-in-law, who delivers them almost daily. Any surplus ends up being used at the restaurant.

Surprisingly, although scarlet runners are a stunning bean to eat, many growers never think of cooking them. With its pretty orange flowers, the bean is sometimes grown as an ornamental to cover ugly garden areas.

They take a bit longer to cook than the conventional round runner bean or the flat green bean, but I urge you to check out growers' markets or ask your local market to get them for you. After all, my mother-in-law can't supply everyone.

The beans also require more trimming than conventional beans and are at their best steamed, then tossed in unsalted butter with salt, freshly ground black pepper and a touch of lemon juice.

The scarlet runner, also known as a pole bean, is prolific and grows from midsummer through February and into early March. They get their name from the rosy-pink hue that surrounds the seeds within the wavy pods, which can grow up to 30-centimetres long. The pink colouring turns grey with age and they can then be cooked in the same way as lima beans.

... Salad of Scarlet Runner Beans with Tomatoes, Almonds and Sweet Onion Vinaigrette / continued

I have been making this foolproof recipe for so many years that it feels like an old friend.

Ingredients / Serves 4

Sweet Onion Vinaigrette
Makes 1 cup

100g red onion, chopped
2 tsp dry mustard powder
a pinch of salt
2 tsp sugar
freshly ground black pepper
125ml olive oil

Salad

500g scarlet runner beans, trimmed
4 tomatoes, seeded and chopped
4 tbsp slivered almonds, lightly toasted
salt and freshly ground black pepper
160ml sweet onion vinaigrette

Method

To make the dressing, put a litre of cold water and the chopped onion in a saucepan and bring it to the boil. Cook for one minute, then drain the onion in a colander under cold running water. Allow to drain thoroughly, then transfer the onion to a blender with the mustard, salt, sugar and a little pepper. Blend until the mixture is creamy and smooth. Keep the motor running and slowly add the oil, which will form a smooth emulsion. Check the seasoning. The dressing should be a soft pink. Transfer to a jar and refrigerate until required.

To make the salad, bring a large pot of salted water to the boil. (This is the best time to get the seasoning into the beans so use plenty of salt.) Cook the beans for four minutes or until tender. Place in a colander under cold running water. Drain thoroughly and then slice into one-centimetre wide diagonal pieces. Place the beans, tomatoes and almonds in a bowl. Gently toss and season lightly.

To Serve

Pile the salad into the centre of a large serving plate and drizzle with the sweet onion vinaigrette.

Light Meals.

Sometimes you want a little more than bread and cheese as a snack. Not that there is anything wrong with bread and cheese, but you need a meal that will stave off hunger pangs, be quick to throw together and made of fresh ingredients plus a few other bits and pieces you already have in the cupboard or fridge. These are the sorts of meals that are realistically achievable and reflect how most of us live. Easy to eat, a light meal is ideal for lunch, snacks or simple dinners — the sort of dish that can be made around a game of 500 or when unexpected guests turn up. Most of all a light meal should stop you ordering out for pizza and get you to spend 30 minutes in the kitchen instead.

This Section

Toasted Baguette, Goat's Cheese, Roasted Garlic and Green Olive Tapenade **80**

Wrap of Soft-boiled Egg, Rocket and Sweet Herb Dressing **83**

Barbecued Pork Sandwich with Homemade Barbecue Sauce and Coleslaw **88**

The Perfect Steak Sandwich **91**

Asparagus with Prosciutto and Parmesan **92**

Eggs Poached in Red Wine **95**

Double-baked Mussel Soufflé with Parsley Sauce **96**

Double-baked Whitebait Soufflé **98**

Whitebait Fritters **100**

Sautéed Whitebait **103**

Pan-roasted Scallops and Crispy Potatoes with Asparagus and Anchovy Butter **104**

Grilled Crayfish with Thyme Butter and Warm Potato Salad **106**

Grilled Fish, Smoked Eel and Potato Salad with Horseradish Cream **109**

Cedar-planked Salmon with Celeriac and Apple Remoulade **110**

Ceviche with Pickled Rock Melon and Pine Nut Vinaigrette **113**

Raw Fish with Sashimi Dressing and Cherry Tomato Salad **115**

Spaghetti, Cockles and Fresh Tomato Sugo **116**

Steamed Cockles, Potato Gnocchi, Anchovies and Olive Oil **118**

Fettuccine with Poached Oysters and Broad Beans **121**

Scarlet Runner Beans with Pasta and Blue Cheese Cream **122**

Miso-braised Pork Belly with Prawns and White Beans **124**

Lamb's Tongue Rillete with Duck Liver Parfait, Grilled Prawn and Salsa Verde **126**

Baked Prosciutto-wrapped Globe Artichokes and Broad Bean Purée with Red Capsicum Oil **129**

Carpaccio of Zucchini, Parmesan, Olive Oil and Lemon Juice **130**

Toasted Baguette, Goat's Cheese, Roasted Garlic and Green Olive Tapenade —

A great late-night supper accompanied by a glass of riesling, this sandwich also makes the perfect aperitif snack. You can adapt this recipe as a small tapas item, serving the cheese and tapenade on thin slices of toasted bread. For lunch, add a salad of lightly dressed green leaves, tomatoes and green beans.

Ingredients / Serves 6

Roasted Garlic

6 whole heads of garlic

180ml olive oil

4 sprigs fresh thyme

2 bay leaves

2 sprigs fresh rosemary

1 lemon

salt and freshly ground black pepper

Green Olive Tapenade
Makes 2 cups

500g green olives, pitted

1 clove garlic

100g anchovy fillets in oil

2 tbsp capers

3 tbsp olive oil

pepper

Baguette

2 baguettes, cut in thirds and sliced in half lengthways

olive oil to brush baguette slices

200g soft-curd goat's cheese

roasted garlic cloves

2 tbsp green olive tapenade

extra olive oil for drizzling

Method

To roast the garlic, preheat the oven to 200°C. Slice the garlic heads in half and place in a deep ovenproof dish. Pour in all the oil and sprinkle the herbs over the top. Cut the lemon in half and squeeze the juice over the garlic. Season with salt and pepper. Bake the garlic in the oven for 10 minutes, then reduce the heat to 170°C and cook for a further 45 minutes. The cloves should be creamy and soft. Remove from the oven and set aside until required.

To make the tapenade, blend all the ingredients in a food processor for five minutes. Store in a jar in the refrigerator. It will keep in the refrigerator for three months.

To prepare the baguette, reheat the oven to 200°C. Brush the cut halves of the baguette with oil and place on a flat baking sheet. Bake for 10–15 minutes until golden. Mash the cheese in a bowl until it's as smooth as possible. In a separate bowl, squeeze the garlic pulp out of the skins and lightly mix. Smear the bread with garlic, cheese and some tapenade before drizzling with a little olive oil to finish.

Wrap of Soft-boiled Egg, Rocket and Sweet Herb Dressing —

Everyone knows the simple pleasure of that ultimate comfort food the boiled egg, but there's so much more you can do with this versatile ingredient.

I remember sitting in a Paris café many years ago, eating eggs mayonnaise for lunch. They had been soft-boiled, carefully peeled and were sitting on a thick slice of buttery toasted baguette, surrounded by bitter leaves of curly endive and coated with mayonnaise and a dusting of cayenne pepper. Behind me on the wall was a plaque bearing Simone de Beauvoir's name; apparently I was sitting in her seat. I was impressed to find such a simple dish on the menu and I tried to recreate it on my return to Wellington. However, it did not sell well. Maybe the dish was just too simple for Kiwi tastes.

Yet many of us will have memories of the pleasure of a hard-boiled egg dipped in salt and ground black pepper and eaten as a solitary late-night supper or possibly as the first restorative taken after an illness. I eat eggs soft-boiled with variations of the toast soldier, such as blue-cheese rind topped with a little apple sauce or melted cheddar cheese on toast, cut into fingers and sprinkled with fresh thyme leaves. If I have any black olives, I might chop up some and sprinkle them on top of the yolk, to be stirred in as I eat.

Ingredients / Serves 6

Wrap

6 eggs

1 tsp celery salt

1 bunch wild rocket

½ cucumber, halved and sliced

6 tortilla wraps or flatbreads

Sweet Herb Dressing
Makes 2 cups

200ml walnut or avocado oil

200ml grapeseed or rice bran oil

1 tsp Dijon mustard

2 shallots, chopped

juice of 2 lemons

90ml white wine vinegar

2 bay leaves

1 tbsp chopped tarragon

1 tbsp chopped chervil

1 tbsp chopped basil

1 tbsp chopped dill

1 tbsp chopped chives

1 tsp sugar

1 whole egg

salt and freshly ground black pepper

Method

Bring a pot of water to a rolling boil. Gently lower the eggs into it and cook for four minutes. Run the eggs under cold running water until cool enough to handle, then peel, taking care to keep them whole. Sprinkle the eggs lightly with celery salt.

To make the dressing, mix the oils and set aside. In a food processor, blend the remaining ingredients until smooth, stopping the machine occasionally to scrape down the sides. With the motor running, add the combined oils in a thin stream until a smooth dressing forms. Season with salt and pepper.

To Serve

Pile some rocket leaves and cucumber onto the wrap. Break the egg over the cucumber and spread it down the length of the wrap. Spoon liberal amounts of sweet herb dressing on the egg and roll up the wrap tightly. Slice in thirds and serve.

Wrap of Soft-boiled Egg,
Rocket and Sweet Herb
Dressing
Recipe on page 83

**Barbecued Pork Sandwich
with Homemade Barbecue
Sauce and Coleslaw**
Recipe on page 88

Barbecued Pork Sandwich with Homemade Barbecue Sauce and Coleslaw —

Whenever I'm barbecuing, my enthusiasm gets the better of me and I prepare a ridiculous amount of food. This results in a number of untouched dishes, much to my wife's vexation, so it makes sense to use the leftovers in sandwiches. In summer sandwiches are likely to make regular appearances, either to ease a child's hunger pangs or to satisfy my own greed. I could write pages about what to put in a sandwich, but the filling is less important than the dressing, or edible 'glue', that brings all the components together. The following recipe is not so much about the sandwich as the parts that help to make it an edible work of art …

The barbecue sauce can be used with anything, and it keeps well in the refrigerator. The apple in the slaw works with the pork, as does the sweet mealiness of the hazelnuts.

Ingredients / Serves 8

Barbecue Sauce

1 tsp dry mustard powder
1 tsp cider vinegar
1 tsp horseradish sauce
1 tsp Worcestershire sauce
1 cup tomato sauce
3 tbsp molasses
3 level tbsp brown sugar
½ cup water
1 small onion, finely chopped

Red Wine Vinegar Dressing
Makes 3 cups

1 small red onion, finely chopped
750ml water
2 tbsp red wine vinegar
1 tsp dry mustard powder
salt and freshly ground black pepper
125ml olive oil

Coleslaw

¼ green cabbage, finely shredded
1 fennel bulb, washed, trimmed and finely sliced
2 carrots, peeled and grated
1 Granny Smith apple, thinly sliced
120g hazelnuts, lightly toasted and roughly chopped
red wine vinegar dressing
salt and freshly ground black pepper

The Sandwich

800g cooked pork
barbecue sauce
8 bread rolls
unsalted butter, softened
coleslaw

Method

To make the barbecue sauce, combine the ingredients in a heavy-based saucepan and simmer over a very low heat for 30 minutes. Strain through a sieve, discarding the solids. The sauce can be used hot or cold. It will keep in the refrigerator for three months.

To make the dressing, bring the onion and water to the boil in a saucepan, then drain. (This process removes the bitterness from the onion.) Discard the liquid and transfer the onion to a food processor with the vinegar, mustard powder and salt and pepper. Blend until creamy and slowly add the oil until the mixture is smooth.

To make the coleslaw, place the cabbage, fennel, carrot, apple and nuts in a bowl. Add the dressing and season with salt and pepper. Gently toss and set aside until required.

To Serve

Use forks to tear the pork into chunks. Gently mix the meat with some of the barbecue sauce to moisten it. Cut the bread rolls in half and spread lightly with butter. Grill the cut sides of the bread until golden brown then remove from the heat. Top with coleslaw and divide the meat between the rolls. Serve with extra sauce on the side.

The Perfect Steak Sandwich —

Among the topics that chefs regularly obsess about is what we eat when we get home late at night. One chef I know tried to perfect the 30-minute trifle. There is, however, a theme to these meals — a bowl of cereal or variations on a cheese toasted sandwich. But why settle for cereal when you can quickly assemble the perfect steak sandwich?

A steak sandwich needs to be many things. The meat should be cooked in foaming butter until rare, but must be well caramelised; the onions should be fried in the pan after the steak is cooked; the toast must be dripping in mayonnaise; peppery rocket leaves should be used over any other variety of green; and the tomatoes must be ripe and flavoursome. Pesto is optional, but I love it. For a truly satisfying sandwich, though, it must be topped with a fried egg with a runny yolk …

Ingredients / Serves 1

3 tbsp olive oil
150g beef fillet, scotch steak or eye of rump
2 tbsp unsalted butter
salt and freshly ground black pepper
1 small onion, finely sliced
1 egg
2 thick slices of bread
1 tbsp mayonnaise
½ cup rocket leaves
1 ripe tomato, sliced thickly
1 tbsp basil pesto

Method

Heat a frying pan and add the oil. Fry the steak on one side until nicely caramelised, then add half the butter and turn the steak over to finish cooking. Baste the steak with the pan juices as it cooks. Season with salt and pepper and remove the steak to a plate to rest, but keep it warm. Add the onion to the pan and cook until golden brown, scraping up any leftover bits of meat. Season lightly with salt and pepper. Remove the onion from the pan and place it on top of the steak. Add the remaining butter to the pan and fry the egg until cooked. Remove it from the pan and place on top of the onion.

To Serve

Toast the bread and spread with mayonnaise. Top with rocket and tomato slices and smear with pesto. Place the steak on top of all this, then complete with the remaining slice of toast. Bliss!

Asparagus with Prosciutto and Parmesan —

I am an advocate of eating seasonally, and I cannot understand why exorbitantly priced imported asparagus is available during our winter months, especially as it has such little flavour. Asparagus arrives with spring and that's when it should be eaten. It's as if we turn a culinary corner in the year, and I make the most of it because asparagus has such a short season. Nothing could be simpler than this to make the most of fresh asparagus. Adding a poached egg to this dish perks it up considerably with its sunny, bright colour and it makes a rich dipping sauce for the asparagus spears.

Ingredients / Serves 6

30 plump asparagus spears, trimmed and peeled

2 tbsp unsalted butter, softened

18 thin slices prosciutto

120g Parmesan cheese

5 tbsp extra virgin olive oil

sea salt and freshly ground black pepper

Method

Bring a large pot of salted water to a rolling boil, add the asparagus and cook for three to four minutes. Remove the hot asparagus to a large bowl with the butter and toss the asparagus around until it is well coated. Place the asparagus on a serving platter and pile the prosciutto loosely on top. Use a vegetable peeler to make thin shavings of Parmesan cheese. Sprinkle these on top and drizzle with oil. Season lightly with sea salt and pepper.

Eggs Poached in Red Wine —

The first time I made eggs poached in red wine was at catering college. We used Velluto Rosso wine from a cask, the sauce was overly thick and lumpy, and the eggs hard from overcooking. Years later I decided to revisit all my early culinary horrors to see if I had misunderstood those dishes. This was one, roasted capsicums was another. Now I love this dish, and it makes a great supper.

Ingredients / Serves 4

12 slices crusty baguette

1 tbsp butter for frying

1 bottle pinot noir

200ml beef stock

1 sprig fresh thyme

1½ tbsp unsalted butter

1 tbsp flour

salt and freshly ground black pepper

8 slices streaky bacon

1 tbsp unsalted butter

25ml red wine vinegar

8 eggs

2 tbsp chopped fresh thyme leaves to garnish

Method

In a hot pan, fry the baguette slices in butter until golden brown. Set aside. Bring three-quarters of the wine to a boil, then cook until the alcohol has evaporated. To test this, deeply inhale the steam coming off the wine — if you get an instant headache, it hasn't evaporated. Add the stock and thyme and reduce by three-quarters. Strain the sauce and return it to the pan. Mix 1½ tablespoons of butter with the flour and thicken the sauce by whisking in small pieces at a time. Season to taste and keep it warm. Cut the bacon into thin strips and fry in one tablespoon of butter until golden brown. Remove the bacon and drain on absorbent paper. Keep it warm. In a separate shallow pan, bring the vinegar and remaining wine to a simmer. Break the eggs individually, place in the pan and gently poach. Lift out with a slotted spoon.

To Serve

Divide the baguette pieces between four plates and top with two eggs each. Divide up the bacon. Pour the sauce over the eggs and sprinkle with thyme leaves.

Double-baked Mussel Soufflé with Parsley Sauce —

Double baking soufflés completely takes away the stress of making them. This method practically guarantees success and leaves you no chance of bringing something fallen and tragic to the table. The soufflés might appear a bit sad to begin with, but they come dazzlingly back to life, looking puffy and golden, on the second baking.

Ingredients / Serves 4

Soufflé

600g mussels
100ml mussel stock (made from steaming open the mussels)
300ml milk
120g unsalted butter
45g flour
1 cup cooked mussels, chopped
4 egg yolks
1 tsp Dijon mustard
salt and freshly ground black pepper
5 egg whites

Parsley Sauce

1 cup white wine
2 cups cream
2 tbsp finely chopped parsley
salt and freshly ground black pepper

Method

Preheat the oven to 180°C. Clean the mussels and pull away any of the beard that is visible. Discard any that have broken shells. Place the mussels in a deep pot with more than 100ml of water. Cover tightly with a lid and steam the mussels for three to four minutes, just long enough for their shells to open, then remove each mussel from its shell. Strain the cooking liquor through a sieve and stir 100ml of it into the milk. In a separate pan heat the butter until it melts and stir in the flour over a low heat. Cook until the mixture resembles a sandy texture and then gradually add the mussel and milk stock, stirring until it is quite smooth. Cook until it thickens, about 10 minutes. Beat in the chopped mussels, the egg yolks and Dijon mustard, remove from the heat and season with the salt and pepper. This base mixture can be made in advance and stored in the refrigerator for three days.

When you are ready to make the soufflé, butter and flour four soufflé ramekins and place them into a deep roasting dish. Whisk the whites of the egg until they resemble soft peaks, and tip half of them into the mussel mixture. Using a metal spoon cut the whites into the mixture, rotating the bowl as you go. Add the remainder of the whites folding them carefully; the mixture should look bubbly and light when finished. Quickly divide the mixture between the prepared ramekins. Place the roasting dish in the centre of the oven and pour in enough hot water to come up the sides of the ramekins, then bake for 30–35 minutes. Remove from the oven and allow the soufflés to cool in the ramekins before turning them out. The soufflés can be prepared in advance and stored in the refrigerator for two days.

To make the parsley sauce, bring the white wine to the boil in a small saucepan and reduce it by half, then add the cream and parsley. Bring to the boil again and season. Place the soufflés into a shallow ovenproof dish and spoon the cream sauce over. Return the soufflés to the oven for five to 10 minutes, until the sauce is bubbling and has thickened nicely. Serve with parsley sauce spooned over the top.

Double-baked Whitebait Soufflé —

From simple recipes to the more elaborate, eggs can be used in an astounding number of ways, either as a meal or as a support act for other dishes. Always buy the freshest eggs, preferably free range. Store eggs pointed-end down in the carton in the refrigerator, as this will prevent air damage. A little understanding of the egg and its properties can help us to perfect cooking them. With soufflés, or meringues, we want to trap the air inside the soft peaks of whipped egg whites and allow it to expand with heat before setting.

Ingredients / Serves 6

300ml milk
100ml chicken stock
2 tbsp unsalted butter
3 tbsp flour
4 eggs, separated
300g whitebait
1 tsp Dijon mustard
sea salt and freshly ground black pepper
300ml cream

Method

Heat the oven to 180°C. Grease and flour small soufflé moulds or breakfast cups. Heat the milk and stock together, but do not boil. In a separate pan, melt the butter and add the flour. Cook over a low heat for about five minutes until the mixture is of a sandy texture and colour. Pour in the hot milk and stock, whisking continuously, and cook until the mixture is smooth and thick. Remove from the heat. Add the egg yolks, whitebait, mustard and seasonings. Whisk the egg whites until stiff peaks form, then fold in the whitebait mixture one-third at a time. Pour the mixture into the prepared moulds and place in a roasting dish. Fill the dish two-thirds with hot water and bake the soufflés for 30 minutes. Remove from the oven and allow them to cool slightly before turning out. Cover and refrigerate. To reheat, place them into a deep dish and pour over the cream. Place in the oven for 15 minutes until the soufflés have risen. Serve, spooning the bubbling cream sauce over them.

Whitebait Fritters —

I learnt how to cook whitebait when I was working at Le Normandie restaurant in Wellington. During each whitebait season, the restaurant owner bought enough to fill a large chest freezer, and that was all we sold.

With only the head chef and myself to do the cooking, we had to be highly organised. For each service we set up large drum sieves, mixing bowls, trays of eggs and a bucket of flour. Lemon halves to garnish the plates were wrapped in muslin, and a large bowl of peeled garlic cloves wobbled precariously on the edge of the stove. By the end of each service, I was covered in flour, with eggshells littering the floor and the stove covered in crispy threads of egg and the odd fish that had escaped the pans.

Ingredients / Serves 4

50–70ml clarified butter
400g whitebait
1 cup flour
sea salt
4 eggs
juice of 1 lemon

Method

To make your own clarified butter for frying the fritters, melt 100g unsalted butter in a microwave set on high for three minutes. Pour off the clear, golden liquid, discarding the white milk solids at the bottom. Unused clarified butter will keep in the refrigerator for many weeks.

Lightly dust the whitebait in enough flour so that each fish is individually coated, then lightly season with the sea salt. Beat the eggs in a separate bowl and pour just enough onto the floured whitebait to bind it. Heat the frying pan and add one tablespoon of the butter. When the butter is hot, pour in one-quarter of the mixture. Cook for about three minutes each side. Repeat three times. Squeeze a little lemon juice over the fritters before serving.

Sautéed Whitebait —

Sautéeing whitebait is my preference. First, I lightly dust the fish with flour before putting it into a hot frying pan. Use a large frying pan to allow plenty of room for the whitebait to brown, otherwise it can become floury and gluggy. If you don't have a large pan, cook the fish in two smaller batches, wiping the pan clean between each round. Never use pepper when seasoning as the flavour is too harsh. The end result is a pile of deliciously crispy and tender fish.

Ingredients / Serves 4

400g whitebait, drained

2 cups plain flour

50–70ml clarified butter

2 cloves garlic, lightly crushed

½ tsp sea salt

juice of 1 lemon

Method

Heat a large frying pan until very hot. Place the drained whitebait in a large sieve and hold it over a roasting dish while liberally dusting the fish with the flour, shaking the sieve to ensure that all are evenly coated. Keep scooping the excess flour from the roasting pan and shaking it over the fish. Do not be tempted to stir the fish with your fingers as this will result in a sticky mess. Once all the fish are lightly coated, add the butter and garlic to the pan. When the butter is hot, quickly remove the garlic and carefully sprinkle the whitebait evenly into the pan. Fry for 30 seconds before using kitchen tongs to gently move the whitebait around the pan. You want the flour to form a toasted crust around the succulent fish. Season with sea salt and a squeeze of lemon juice and remove the fish from the pan. Drain on kitchen paper before dividing the whitebait between four plates.

Pan-roasted Scallops and Crispy Potatoes with Asparagus and Anchovy Butter —

Thick slices of potato — sautéed until crisp in foaming butter — with scallops and asparagus are a heavenly combination of textures and have terrific flavours in each bite.

Ingredients / Serves 4

20 asparagus spears

4 tbsp unsalted butter, melted, or olive oil

12 gourmet potatoes, cooked and cut into 5-mm-thick rounds

sea salt

24–30 scallops (depending on the size)

juice of 1 lemon

3 tbsp anchovy butter (see page 257)

2 tsp chopped chives to garnish

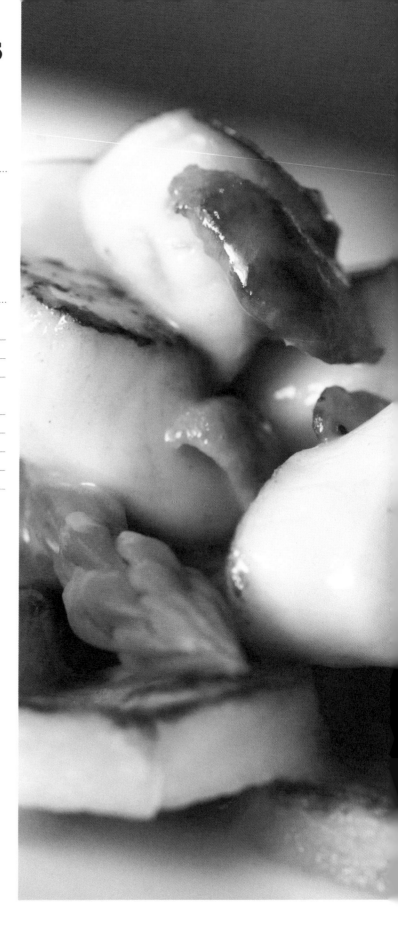

Method

Bring a large pot of salted water to a rolling boil and plunge in the asparagus. Cook for a maximum of three minutes until just tender. Remove the asparagus from the water, drain on a wet tea towel, then roll it up to keep it warm. In a large frying pan, heat two tablespoons of butter and cook the potatoes until crisp. Season lightly with salt and pepper. Drain on absorbent kitchen paper and keep in a warm place.

Wipe the frying pan clean and return it to the heat. Put the scallops into a bowl and mix with the remaining melted butter until they are well coated. Carefully add the scallops to the hot pan and cook until golden brown. Season with salt and a squeeze of lemon juice, then remove from the pan and lower the heat. Add the anchovy butter to the pan and let it melt slowly while stirring through the pan juices.

Grilled Crayfish with Thyme Butter and Warm Potato Salad —

I love the simplicity of cooking food in its own 'container' — corn cooked in its husk for example. Crayfish cooked in its shell is another; it intensifies the sea flavours and concentrates the sugars.

Ingredients / Serves 4

Warm Potato Salad

8 Jersey Benne or new season potatoes

1 tbsp olive oil

1 cup sour cream

juice of 1 lemon

2 tbsp capers, rinsed and chopped

½ bunch chives, finely chopped

½ bunch chervil, finely chopped

salt and freshly ground black pepper

Grilled Crayfish

1 crayfish, split in half lengthways

100g thyme butter (see page 257)

salt

juice of 1 lemon

salad leaves

Method

To make the salad, first wash the potatoes. Place them in a deep saucepan, cover with hot water and bring to a trembling simmer. Once cooked, drain and leave until cool enough to handle. Remove the skins. Combine the oil, sour cream, lemon juice, capers and herbs to make a dressing. Slice the potatoes and fold in the dressing. Season with salt and pepper.

To cook the crayfish, place it shell side down on a hot barbecue plate and continuously baste the cut side with thyme butter for six to eight minutes, until the translucent flesh starts to turn white. Turn the crayfish over and cook until the meat is a golden-brown colour, about four minutes. Remove to a plate shell-side down, season with salt and a little lemon juice.

To Serve

Place the potato salad in the centre of a large platter. Remove the meat from the crayfish tail and chop it into three-centimetre chunks. Scatter the salad leaves around the platter and place the crayfish on top of the potato salad. Serve the bodies and legs of the crayfish as well.

Grilled Fish, Smoked Eel and Potato Salad with Horseradish Cream —

I use snapper for this because of the way it flakes into the potatoes as you cut into it and mixes with the smoked eel.

Ingredients / Serves 4

400g potatoes, peeled and chopped

200g smoked eel fillets

1 tbsp chopped chives

1 tbsp horseradish cream

120ml crème fraîche

zest of 1 orange

salt and freshly ground black pepper

800g firm white-fleshed fish fillets

2 tbsp unsalted butter, melted

salt

juice of 1 lemon

Method

To make the potato salad, put the potatoes in a saucepan and bring to the boil. Cook until they are tender when pierced with the tip of a sharp knife. When the potatoes are cooked, drain them in a colander. Do not run cold water over them — leave them to cool on their own. Chop the smoked eel into one-centimetre cubes. In a large bowl mix the cooled potatoes with the eel and chives. Combine the horseradish and crème fraîche together with the orange zest and toss gently through the potatoes and eel. Season with salt and pepper.

To cook the fish, preheat the grill. Place the portions of fish on a shallow baking sheet and brush with the melted butter. Put the fish under the grill and cook for three minutes. Turn the fish, season with salt and cook for a further three minutes depending on the thickness of the fillets. Remove the fish to a plate, add the lemon juice and keep it warm.

To Serve

Divide the potato salad between individual plates and top with a piece of the grilled fish.

Cedar-planked Salmon with Celeriac and Apple Remoulade —

Although this recipe for cedar-planked salmon was never really mine, it has been widely attributed to me. It has always brought great joy to those who eat it.

Ingredients / Serves 4

Salmon

sea salt

4 pieces of dressed untreated
14cm x 7cm cedar plank

4 x 100g salmon fillets

1 tsp soft brown sugar

1 tsp dry mustard powder

50g melted butter to garnish

a squeeze of lemon juice to garnish

2 tbsp chopped chives or fresh thyme
leaves to garnish

Celeriac and Apple Remoulade

200ml mayonnaise

1½ tsp grain mustard

grated zest and juice of ½ lemon

1 medium celeriac

1 Granny Smith apple

salt and freshly ground black pepper

Method

To prepare the salmon, lightly sprinkle some sea salt over the pieces of cedar. Place a piece of salmon on top of each one, trimming the fillets if necessary to fit the planks. Check the fish for bones, using small pliers or tweezers to gently remove any. Lightly season the salmon with sea salt. It is important to do the next two steps in order. First, rub the soft brown sugar onto the top of the fillet. Sieve the mustard powder over the sugar. It doesn't matter if any of the sugar or mustard ends up on the wood, as it will caramelise around the salmon and become part of the delicious juices.

Place the planks on top of the grill bars of the barbecue and cover them with an upturned metal container. (I use an old roasting pan.) The wood needs only to smoulder, not burst into flames. Check the salmon after five minutes. It is cooked when small white beads of cooked protein form on the outside. Mix the melted butter with a squeeze of lemon juice and the chopped chives or fresh thyme leaves. When the fish is ready to serve, pour some of this mixture over the top.

To make the remoulade, mix the mayonnaise, mustard, lemon zest and juice. Slice the ends off the celeriac and use a sharp knife to peel away the thick skin. Split the celeriac in half lengthways. Place each half flat side down on a chopping board and cut into very fine semi-circular slices. Slice these into matchsticks. Add to the dressing. Peel the apple and remove the two cheeks from either side of the core. Repeat as for the celeriac and also add to the dressing. Season with the salt and pepper and mix well.

To Serve

Spoon the salad onto four individual plates. Serve a piece of salmon alongside, preferably on the smoking plank.

Ceviche with Pickled Rock Melon and Pine Nut Vinaigrette —

I like to use firm white-fleshed fish, such as blue cod or snapper, for this refreshingly light salad.

Ingredients / Serves 4

Ceviche

450g white fish fillets, skinned and boned

juice of 2 limes

1 small red onion, finely chopped

1 tbsp finely chopped chives

1 tbsp finely chopped coriander leaves

Pickled Rock Melon

½ rock melon, peeled and seeded

3 tbsp white wine vinegar

2 tbsp sugar

Pine Nut Vinaigrette
Makes 1 cup

1 red capsicum, deseeded and finely chopped

1 small cucumber, peeled and finely sliced

1 small red onion, finely chopped

2 cloves garlic, finely chopped

1 tsp Dijon mustard

3 tbsp pinenuts, lightly toasted

zest and juice of 1 orange

2 tbsp olive oil

salt and freshly ground black pepper

Method

To prepare the ceviche, slice the fish thinly into five-millimetre pieces and mix with the other ingredients. Marinate for no more than 45 minutes.

To pickle the rock melon, place the melon cut side down on a chopping board and slice it into three-millimetre half-moon shapes. Place these into a deep container. In a small saucepan bring the vinegar and sugar to a lazy simmer and cook for two minutes, until the sugar is dissolved. Remove from the heat and cool. Pour the syrup over the melon 30 minutes before serving.

To make the vinaigrette, combine the capsicum, cucumber, red onion, garlic and mustard in a small bowl. Stir in the pinenuts with the orange zest and juice and whisk in the olive oil. Season with salt and pepper.

To Serve

Place a pile of marinated fish in the centre of a plate and arrange the pickled melon on top. Drizzle the pine nut vinaigrette over the fish and serve immediately. Garnish with small salad leaves or picked herbs.

Raw Fish with Sashimi Dressing and Cherry Tomato Salad —

Thanks to Japanese cuisine, eating raw fish has become more acceptable to us all. From sashimi to paper-thin carpaccio of tuna to chopped tartares of salmon, raw fish features on menus everywhere. It's clean, fresh, healthy and pure and does not need many other flavours to enhance it. Freshness is key to eating raw fish, so take the time to seek out the best quality. I like to serve a large platter of thinly sliced raw fish drizzled with this dressing, placing it on the table for my guests to help themselves.

The dressing, which keeps in the refrigerator for months, is perfect to leave at the bach or on the boat for when you next catch a fish. I keep some nearby when I'm preparing seafood to dip off-cuts of fish, oysters or scallops to snack on as I go. It also works well with grilled lamb or beef.

Ingredients / Serves 4

Sashimi Dressing
Makes approximately 1 cup

175g onion, finely chopped

125ml soy sauce

115ml rice wine vinegar

100ml water

½ tsp sugar

1 tbsp dry mustard powder

freshly ground black pepper

50ml grapeseed oil

50ml sesame oil

Fish

120g fresh salmon fillets, skinned and boned

120g fresh white fish fillets (such as groper, snapper or blue cod)

120g fresh tuna or kingfish fillets

Cherry Tomato Salad

1 punnet of cherry tomatoes

1 tbsp olive oil

1 tbsp sesame oil

1 tbsp rice wine vinegar

1 tsp sugar

salt and freshly ground black pepper

fresh herbs to garnish, such as tarragon, chervil or parsley

Method

To make the dressing, combine the onion, soy sauce, rice wine vinegar, water and sugar together and stir until the sugar has dissolved. Whisk in the remaining ingredients and strain the dressing, discarding the onion. Keep it in the refrigerator and before using, allow it to come back to room temperature and then give it a good shake.

To prepare the fish, slice the fillets thinly into three-millimetre pieces on a slight bias across the grain. You may need to cut the salmon and tuna in half lengthways before you do this. Arrange the fish on a platter, alternating the colours. You can marinate the fish in the dressing for 30 minutes, or simply pour it over just before serving, or even place the dressing in a dish on the side, to dip slices of fish into.

To assemble the salad, cut the cherry tomatoes in half. In a small bowl combine all the ingredients, except for the herbs, and season to taste.

To Serve

Place the fish onto one large platter and arrange the tomato salad on the fish and scatter the fresh herbs over the top.

Spaghetti, Cockles and Fresh Tomato Sugo —

Although it's not essential, I prefer to remove the cockles from the shells before adding them to pasta. This is because I want to eat without having to fuss with shells coated in sauce.

Ingredients / Serves 4

Fresh Tomato Sugo

120ml olive oil

2 tbsp finely chopped garlic

1kg ripe tomatoes, skinned and roughly chopped

salt and freshly ground black pepper

Spaghetti and Cockles

400g spaghetti

100g butter

2 tbsp olive oil

2 cloves garlic, finely sliced

1kg cockles

salt

squeeze of lemon juice

Method

To make the sugo, heat the oil in a deep saucepan over a medium setting, and fry the garlic for about three minutes until it begins to turn golden brown. Add the tomatoes and cook for 20 minutes, using a spoon to break them up. Continue cooking until the sauce reduces to a thick consistency. Season with salt and pepper. The sugo can be used immediately. Alternatively, it will keep in the refrigerator for up to seven days.

To cook the pasta, bring a large, deep saucepan of salted water to a rolling boil. Cook the spaghetti for about 12 minutes until tender. Reserve half a cup of the cooking water before draining the spaghetti.

To prepare the cockles, heat the butter and oil in a frying pan until the butter begins to foam but is without colour, then add the garlic. Once the garlic has taken on a little colour, carefully add the reserved pasta water and the cockles. Cover and cook for about seven minutes until the shells open, discarding any that don't. Season with salt and a squeeze of lemon juice. Remove the cockles and set aside. Tip the cooked spaghetti into the pan and stir to combine.

To Serve

Divide the spaghetti between individual bowls, surround with cockles and pour over the sugo.

Steamed Cockles, Potato Gnocchi, Anchovies and Olive Oil —

Although I enjoy making my own gnocchi, I am not such a purist as to insist that only homemade will do. To that end, I usually have a packet of commercial gnocchi in my refrigerator. They are never as cloud-light as the handmade variety, but they are quite acceptable when sautéed in butter to a light golden crust. Add cream if you wish to make this dish a touch more refined.

Ingredients / Serves 4

1kg cockles

½ cup water

1 cup white wine

2 cloves garlic, chopped

1 bay leaf

200g unsalted butter

1 small bunch parsley, chopped

2 cloves garlic, sliced

400g store-bought potato gnocchi

4 anchovies

2 tbsp finely chopped parsley

freshly ground black pepper

100ml olive oil

Method

Put the cockles, water, wine and garlic in a deep saucepan with the bay leaf and 100g of butter. Cover with a lid and steam the cockles for about seven minutes over a medium heat until they open, discarding any that don't. Add the parsley. Shake the saucepan gently to mix all the juices. Remove the cockles and set aside. Reserve a cup of the cooking liquor, and remove the cockles from the shells.

Melt the remaining butter in a frying pan over a medium heat and add the garlic. When it begins to sizzle, add the gnocchi, tossing carefully until it turns a golden colour. Add the anchovies and parsley. Once the anchovies have broken up, add enough of the reserved stock to moisten the gnocchi without swamping it. Add the cockles, and season with pepper.

To Serve

Carefully spoon the mixture into a deep serving platter and drizzle with the oil.

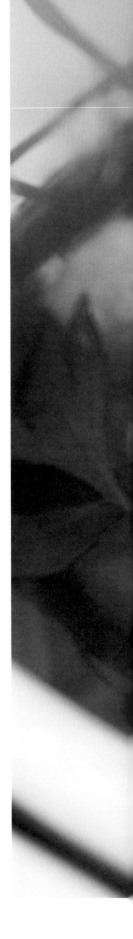

Fettuccine with Poached Oysters and Broad Beans —

Light and easy pasta dishes that use seafood and fresh local ingredients are always a good combination. That said, this is probably the dish to do if you want to show off a bit. After all, how often do you have a dozen oysters in your refrigerator waiting to be used? Double-podding the broad beans doesn't take long — it's actually quite satisfying to do and the result is worth the extra effort.

Ingredients / Serves 4

750g broad beans
200g fettuccine or tagliatelle
2 cloves garlic
1 tbsp olive oil
200ml cream
zest of 1 lemon
12 rock or Pacific oysters, rinsed of grit and sand
1 small bunch of mint
salt and freshly ground black pepper
2 tbsp salmon roe

Method

Shell the beans and plunge into boiling water for six minutes. Run them under cold water, and remove the skins. This is called double-podding. (If the beans are young and tender, you will not need to do this.) You should end up with one cup of beans. Bring a large saucepan of salted water to a rapid boil and add the pasta. Following the packet instructions, cook until tender, then drain. Slice the garlic finely, put it in a frying pan with the oil and cook over a low heat until soft and without colour. Add the cream and bring it to a simmer, then add the lemon zest and oysters. Cook until the oysters tighten slightly. Add the beans. Finely shred the mint leaves and add to the frying pan. Season with salt and black pepper. Add the drained pasta and mix together lightly.

To Serve

Divide the pasta between four individual bowls. Sprinkle some roe on top of each bowl.

Scarlet Runner Beans with Pasta and Blue Cheese Cream —

All this really needs is a simply dressed side salad of peppery rocket leaves, with maybe some ripe cherry tomatoes tossed through it. The recipe relies on the Parmesan and blue cheeses for its saltiness — no added salt is required.

Ingredients / Serves 4

500g scarlet runner beans, trimmed
500g orecchiette or penne-type pasta
2 tbsp unsalted butter
2 tbsp Parmesan cheese, grated
freshly ground black pepper
1 cup cream
150g blue cheese, such as Kapiti Kikorangi or Te Mata Creamy Blue

Method

Bring two saucepans of salted water to the boil. Slice the beans into long, thin strips and cook in one saucepan for three minutes. Drain the beans and set aside to keep warm. Cook the pasta in the other saucepan. Reserve a cup of the cooking water, then drain the pasta and stir in the butter and Parmesan. Season lightly with pepper, then set aside. Return the saucepan to the heat and add the cream. Bring to the boil and cook until it has reduced by half. Add the cup of reserved pasta water and bring back to the boil. Add the blue cheese, reduce the heat and gently stir in the pasta.

To Serve

Arrange the warm beans attractively on top of the pasta.

Miso-braised Pork Belly with Prawns and White Beans —

The miso marinade used here is great with any pork-belly dish as it adds a sweet, malty flavour. I also enjoy combining a luxury ingredient with an inexpensive one and seeing how well two different flavours — the prawns and the pork — marry when cooked. Just think surf 'n' turf or the carpetbag steak with its filling of raw oysters.

Ingredients / Serves 6

Miso Marinade

3 tbsp miso paste

1 tbsp mustard, preferably Dijon-style

3 tbsp mirin (sweet low-alcohol rice wine)

2 tbsp rice wine vinegar

1 tbsp sugar

1.5kg pork belly, skin and bones removed

Braised Pork

1 carrot, peeled and chopped

1 onion, chopped

1 stalk celery, chopped

1 knob of ginger, peeled and sliced

4 cloves garlic, peeled

200ml white wine

2.5 litres water

marinated pork belly

Prawns and White Beans

2 tbsp unsalted butter

18 prawns, peeled

½ head of cabbage, finely sliced

400g can white beans, well rinsed

100g unsalted butter to finish the sauce

Method

To prepare the marinade mix all the ingredients to a smooth paste. Cover the pork with the paste, massaging it in well and refrigerate overnight. The next day, heat the oven to 160°C. Scatter the carrot, onion, celery, ginger and garlic over the base of a shallow roasting pan that is big enough to hold the pork. Pour in the wine and water and bring to a boil on a stovetop element. Place the pork on top and bring it back to the boil, skimming off any foamy surface scum. Cover the pork with greaseproof paper, then tinfoil. Place the pork in the oven and cook for three hours. Remove the pan from the oven and carefully lift the pork out onto a tray. Strain the pan juices into a saucepan and discard the vegetables. Bring the juice to a gentle simmer and let it reduce to a light, syrupy consistency — about 10–15 minutes. While the juices are reducing, use two forks to shred the meat into thick strands. Collect any juices as you go and add to the saucepan.

To prepare the prawns and beans, heat a large frying pan and melt the first measure of butter. Add the prawns and sauté until cooked — about three minutes. Remove the prawns from the pan and add the cabbage. Cook until it has wilted but is still slightly crunchy. Add the beans, pork, prawns and the reduced stock and bring to a simmer. Add the 100g of butter, gently shaking the pan to swirl it through the sauce.

To Serve

Serve in one large bowl or individual bowls.

Lamb's Tongue Rillette with Duck Liver Parfait, Grilled Prawn and Salsa Verde —

Sometimes rustic dishes that are familiar to us can be dressed up in new ways, ready to impress again, or to provide the humble reassurance that comes from known flavours. Corned lamb's tongues are such an ingredient for me. It is now virtually impossible to obtain fresh tongues — I do not know why — so I always have a couple of cans in my cupboard at home. The lamb's tongue is a dish of opposites, where an ingredient such as tongue is transformed into charmingly seductive rillettes and given a degree of dignity with the addition of the prawn and the paté. I love the idea of such juxtaposition between ingredients. The salsa verde gives a pleasant salty contrast. I like to use a crispy fried slice of potato as a base for the rillettes to sit on, but toasted crusty bread will work too.

Ingredients / Serves 4

Lamb's Tongue Rillette

330g can lamb's tongues

30g duck fat

salt and pepper

1 cup cooked spinach, seasoned

Duck Liver Parfait / Serves 8

4 shallots

50ml dry vermouth

5 peppercorns

140ml cream

4 eggs

500g duck livers

500g unsalted butter, melted

Salsa Verde

1 bunch parsley, approx 170g

1 bunch basil, approx 50g

6 anchovies

2 tbsp capers

2 cloves garlic, finely chopped

1 small red onion, chopped

3 tbsp white wine vinegar

3 tbsp olive oil

salt and freshly ground black pepper

Prawns

4 prawns, de-veined

1 tbsp unsalted butter

juice of ½ lemon

salt

Method

To make the rillettes, clean the tongues under running cold water, removing any jelly. Drain and shred the meat with two forks until you are left with fine strands. Soften the duck fat in a small pot over a low heat, then gently stir in the shredded tongue, and season generously with salt and pepper. Line a shallow baking tin with greaseproof paper and press the mixture evenly into it about two-centimetres deep and refrigerate overnight.

Preheat the oven to 180°C. Turn out the rillette mixture and cut into four by two centimetre lengths. Heat a frying pan (that you can put into the

discarding the solids. Return the small pot to a low heat, adding back in the reduced vermouth and warm with the cream. Blend the eggs with the duck livers in a food processor until silky smooth and with the motor running add the warm cream mixture. Then very slowly add the melted butter. Grease and line a terrine mould or bread tin with greaseproof paper. Pour in the duck liver mixture and cover with either tin foil or a lid. Place the mould in a roasting dish and pour in enough hot water to come two-thirds up the sides and carefully slide it into the oven. Cook for 40 minutes. Remove the parfait from the oven and refrigerate overnight.

To make the salsa verde, place all ingredients except the oil in a food processor. Blend to a smooth puree, scraping the sides of the bowl occasionally. Lastly, add the oil in a thin stream, then season carefully with salt and pepper.

To cook the prawns, heat the butter in a frying pan until it foams, then add the prawns. Cook for two minutes until they turn a rosy pink hue and turn them over. Season with lemon juice and salt. Drain the prawns on to absorbent paper.

To Serve

Place some cooked spinach onto each rillette, then top with a prawn and a generous spoonful of the parfait. Spoon some salsa verde on the plate next to the rillette.

oven) over a medium heat and add the slices of rillette. Cook for two minutes and then gently turn the slices over. Place the frying pan into the oven for three minutes. Remove from the oven for serving.

To make the parfait, preheat the oven to 140°C. In a small pot bring the shallots, vermouth and peppercorns to a simmer and reduce liquid to a tablespoon. Strain into a small bowl,

Baked Prosciutto-wrapped Globe Artichokes and Broad Bean Purée with Red Capsicum Oil —

All of these make great individual dishes on their own. The broad bean purée is a fabulous dip, and the red capsicum oil can be used over fish or chicken. Together they are pure Mediterranean flavours — robust and concentrated.

Ingredients / Serves 6

400g jar artichoke hearts, drained

180g prosciutto, thinly sliced

Broad Bean Purée

2kg broad beans

500ml chicken stock

2 tsp fresh thyme leaves

salt and freshly ground black pepper

Red Capsicum Oil
Makes 2 cups

6 red capsicums

olive oil for baking

½ tsp sea salt

300ml olive oil

juice of 3 lemons

Method
To prepare the artichokes, preheat the oven to 180°C. Dry the artichokes and wrap each one in prosciutto.

Place them in a baking dish and bake for 25 minutes.

To make the purée, bring a pot of salted water to the boil. Shell the beans and plunge into boiling water for six minutes. Run them under cold water, and remove the skins. (If the beans are young and tender, you will not need to do this.) You should end up with two cup of beans. Put the beans back into the pot with the stock and thyme. Bring to a gentle simmer and cook for eight minutes. Drain, separating the beans and the liquid. Put the beans into a food processor and use some of the cooking liquid to help create a smooth purée. Season with salt and pepper.

To make the capsicum oil, preheat the oven to 180°C. Rub the capsicums with a small amount of oil, place in a roasting dish and bake until the skins blister — about 20 minutes. Remove from the oven and place in a plastic bag until cool enough to handle. Peel off the skins, then remove the seeds and discard. Slice the flesh of three capsicums into thick strips. Put the remaining capsicums through a juicer. Put the juice into a small saucepan with the sliced capsicum and sea salt. Simmer for 10 minutes, then add the oil and cook for a further 10 minutes. Add the lemon juice and remove from the heat. In a food processor, purée the mixture until smooth.

To Serve
Remove the artichokes from the oven, slice in half and serve on top of the broad bean purée with the capsicum oil spooned around.

Carpaccio of Zucchini, Parmesan, Olive Oil and Lemon Juice —

This is so simple and natural and has a marvellous spontaneity about it.

Ingredients / Serves 4

6 medium zucchini, washed
juice and zest of 1 lemon
3 tbsp olive oil
100g Parmesan cheese
2 tsp chopped fresh thyme leaves
1 tsp chopped parsley
salt and freshly ground black pepper

Method

Top and tail the zucchini and use a potato peeler to cut into long continuous strips. Place them in a bowl. Whisk the lemon juice and oil and combine with the zucchini. Using a potato peeler, make Parmesan shavings and gently mix through the zucchini. Add the herbs. Season lightly with salt and pepper.

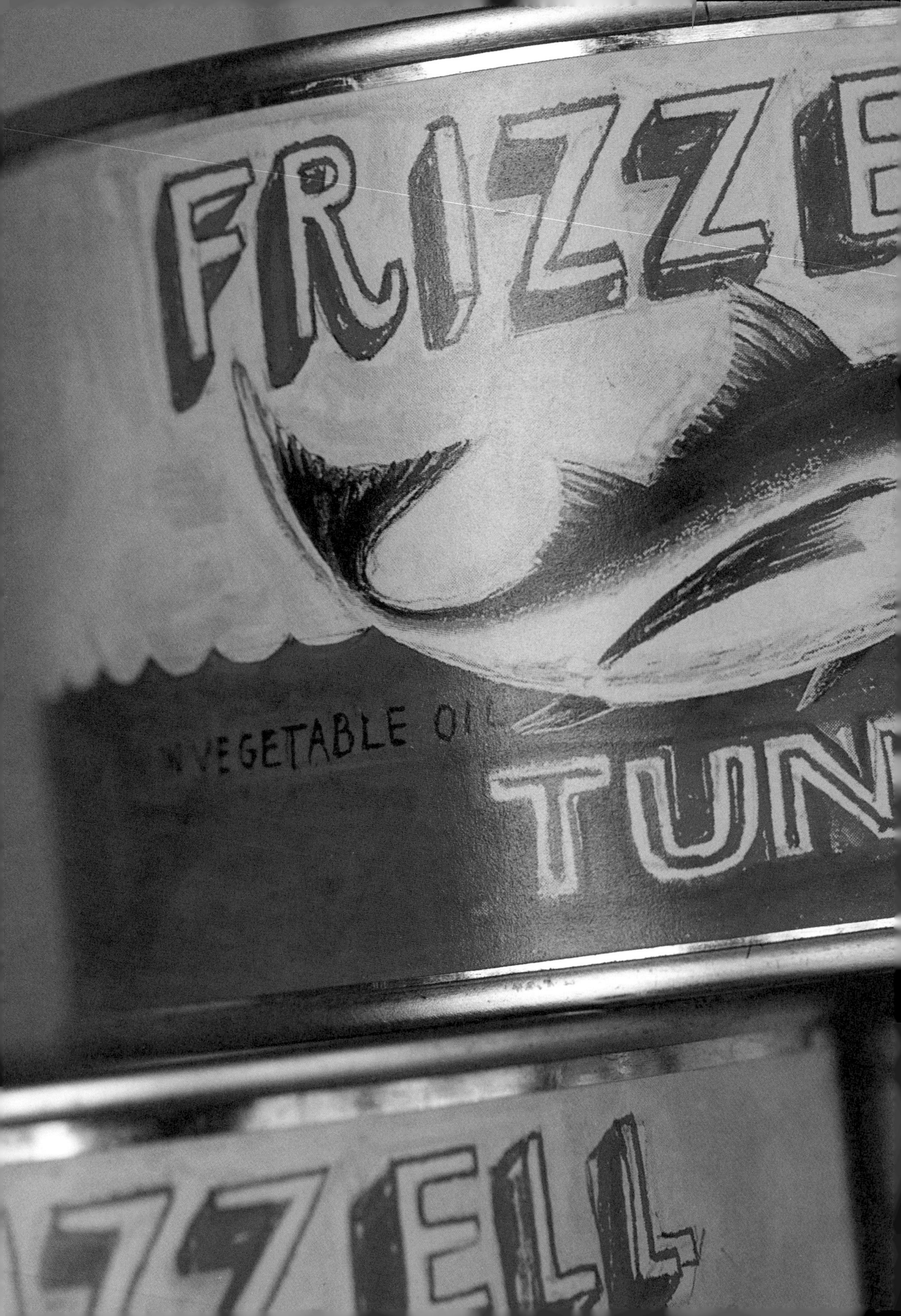
FRIZZE
VEGETABLE OI
TUN
ZZELL

SILVERBEET
99c each

AVOCADO
99c each

25 May | Queen Elizabeth Park

CLOSED TUESDAY
AND WEDNESDAY

Mains.

When you sit down to share food as a family, get together for special occasions or entertain to impress, there's an emotional investment attached to the meal that can bring reflections of past meals, feelings of warmth and sentimentality, and lay down memories for the future. This is one of the pleasures of cooking for others.

Some of the dishes in this section of the book may require extra time or a little more effort when it comes to technique or ingredients, but all are accessible. Some can be made for weeknight family dinners, when you want something a bit more substantial than a one-dish meal. Still others are there to inspire you for when you want to make someone feel special or to commemorate a significant event. And lastly, there are always times when you want to spend hours pottering away in the kitchen putting together your magnus opus, creating your own signature dishes. Cooking should be enjoyable and easy, so for the more complicated dishes I often split the recipe into stages so that a minimum of effort is needed on the day and you can spend time eating and drinking with your guests.

This Section

Basic Risotto — **141**

Cauliflower Risotto — **141**

Cauliflower Couscous, Sautéed with Parmesan Cheese — **142**

Rice Congee with Chicken and Oysters — **144**

Chicken, Potato and Hazelnut Terrine with Asparagus and Sweetcorn Salad — **148**

B'stilla — **151**

Seafood Cassoulet — **153**

Poached Fish with Barbecued Potatoes, Spinach and Black Olive Tapenade — **155**

Grilled Fish and Fresh Peas with Prawn Mashed Potatoes — **156**

Grilled Salmon and Soba Noodle Salad with Rock Sugar Dressing — **158**

Grilled Tuna with Scarlet Runners, Prosciutto and Potato Salad with Caper Dressing — **161**

Grilled Fish with Roast Kumara Purée and Red Wine and Mushroom Ragoût — **162**

Fish Braised with Tomatoes, Mussels and Cockles — **165**

Barbecued Lamb Rump with Charred Vegetables and Anchovy Butter — **166**

Grilled Lamb Rump with Chorizo Sausage, Chickpeas and Mushrooms and Apple and Onion Salad — **169**

Slow-cooked Beef Cheeks, Smoked Eel, Young Carrots with Celeriac Purée — **171**

Beef à la Ficelle — **174**

Grilled Steak with Rosemary and Garlic Fried Potatoes, Green Beans and Reduced Pan Juices — **177**

Pan-fried Fillet Steak with Potato Gnocchi, Prosciutto and Brussel Sprouts and Grain Mustard Sauce — **178**

Braised Short Ribs, Green Olives and Currants with Roast Parsnips and Spinach — **181**

Slow-cooked Pork Belly with Aromatic Spices and Plums — **183**

Bolognese-style Pork Loin Braised in Milk — **184**

Grilled Pork Chops with White Beans, Fennel and Spicy Sausage — **187**

Risotto —

Who said that making beautifully creamy risotto required constant attention, continuous stirring and regular additions of stock?

Nearly 20 years ago, when we opened Brasserie Flipp, I put risotto on the menu. I wanted to make the rich Italian risottos that I had read about and that no one I knew seemed to be cooking. Night after night, guests sent back their lovingly made creamy, Parmesan-laden risottos because the dish wasn't stir-fried with peas and carrots, which was then the norm.

Despondent, I dropped it from the menu a year later, only to be presented with a petition from a small number of guests who wanted a return of the 'Flipp Gluggy Rice'. It's evidence of how far our food culture has come that so many people are now experts in making risotto.

A few years later, I hosted Gabrielle Ferron, the Italian grower of the Carnaroli rice I was using, at a special dinner that featured his own risotto. Despite his apparent lack of English, he was able to dispel many of the risotto-making myths that I had laboured under: that the dish required constant attention, continuous stirring and the addition of the stock, ladle by ladle. Ferron's method involved a long, slow toasting of the rice, after which he added all the stock. This method allows the rice to absorb the liquid without being disturbed by constant stirring.

His method is part of my basic recipe, which will give you perfect risotto in 15–18 minutes. When making risotto, do not wash the rice before cooking as this will remove some of the lovely starch that helps to thicken it. When finished, the risotto should be creamy and loose, and will settle after about 15 seconds.

You can add anything you like to this basic recipe. Use short-grain, Arborio or Carnaroli rice and, if you don't want to use meat stock, use water flavoured with any of the trimmings of the main ingredient you wish to add.

Basic Risotto —

Ingredients / Serves 6

600ml chicken stock
1 tbsp olive oil
2 tbsp unsalted butter
½ cup finely chopped onion
500g Carnaroli or Arborio rice
1 bay leaf
160ml dry white wine or vermouth
salt and freshly ground black pepper
Parmesan cheese to taste

Method

Put the stock into a saucepan and bring it to a gentle simmer. Heat the olive oil in a heavy-bottomed pan. When it is warm, stir in the butter until melted. Add the onion and gently sauté until it is soft and shiny but without colour. Lower the heat and add the rice. Stir continuously to coat all the grains. As the rice gently toasts, it will start to give off delicate nutty and floral aromas. This should take about five minutes. Add the bay leaf, then stir in the white wine or vermouth, continuing to stir until it has been absorbed by the rice. Pour on all the simmering stock, stir well, then cover the pot with a lid. Cook for 13 minutes. Remove the lid and stir the rice. Test a little — it should still be a little firm to the bite. Add the salt and black pepper to taste. At this point, you could serve the risotto, adding Parmesan cheese to taste as you wish. To make it creamier, stir vigorously just before serving. Alternatively, you can add another flavouring and cook the base for a further three minutes.

Cauliflower Risotto —

Ingredients / Serves 6

½ cauliflower, chopped into florets
200ml cream
100ml chicken stock or water
Parmesan cheese to sprinkle
olive oil

Method

Place the cauliflower, cream and stock in a saucepan and bring to a simmer. Cook until the cauliflower is soft and transfer the ingredients to a blender or food processor. Purée until very smooth, then stir into a basic risotto. If you have any uncooked cauliflower left over, grate and stir it through. Sprinkle generously with Parmesan cheese and a drizzle of olive oil, if desired.

Cauliflower Couscous, Sautéed with Parmesan Cheese —

Cauliflower cheese is one of my hero dishes. When it is made well, with a really smooth white sauce and flavoured with Parmesan or Pecorino cheese, it is hard to resist. Cook cauliflower like this, without the white sauce, and it is a meal on its own, which I call couscous, because that is what the crumbs resemble. The anchovy is optional, but provides a wonderful base flavour that underpins the Parmesan cheese flavour.

Ingredients / Serves 4

½ head of cauliflower

100ml olive oil

2 anchovies

2 cloves garlic

2 tbsp chopped parsley

2 tbsp grated Parmesan cheese

salt and freshly ground black pepper

Method

Slice the cauliflower in half from top to bottom. Then lie it on the cut side and slice thinly so that the florets break into small crumbs. Trim around the stalk — you only want to cut the florets. Heat the olive oil in a frying pan and add the anchovies and garlic. Cook until the anchovies melt and the garlic is golden. Scatter over the cauliflower crumbs and stir, turning the mixture from time to time until it is all tender. Sprinkle the parsley and Parmesan cheese through the cauliflower and stir until the cheese melts. Season and serve hot.

Rice Congee with Chicken and Oysters —

This congee is the ultimate restorative with its porridge-like consistency and its flavours of ginger and soy. It is incredibly easy to make, because the object is to overcook the rice, releasing the starch and causing it to thicken. This recipe is an ideal way to use up all the leftover bits of chicken that cling to the carcass after it has been roasted. Congee could well be the new, luxurious comfort food.

Ingredients / Serves 4–6

½ cup short-grain rice

1 litre chicken stock or water

2 tsp chopped garlic

2 tsp chopped ginger

4 tsp soy sauce

4 tbsp fish sauce

1 cooked chicken, shredded, and any reserved juices

12 raw oysters, drained of their juices

1 spring onion, finely sliced on the diagonal

Method

Cook the rice in the stock or water for two hours until it collapses and becomes creamy — it should have a similar texture to porridge. Add the seasonings. Stir in the chicken and some of the juices. Just before serving, add the oysters, heating them through until they are tight and plump. Pour the congee into serving bowls and garnish with spring onion.

Chicken, Potato and Hazelnut Terrine with Asparagus and Sweetcorn Salad —

There is confusion over the difference between a terrine and a pâté. Terrines are glorified meatloaf — they are coarse-textured and robust looking; whereas, pâtés are the smooth-textured, refined and elegant result of an emulsification of meat and fat. Both have delicate flavours and look impressive, and both appear intimidating to make. The truth is that they are not that hard. For instance, a terrine is essentially meatloaf cooked in a mould, although it can also be made in cheesecloth or plastic wrap.

There are several points to remember when making pâtés and terrines:

+ Keep all the ingredients and equipment very cold, otherwise the fat will soften or melt and separate out from the mixture as it cooks, leading to a dry result.
+ Season the mixture well. Food that is to be served chilled needs more seasoning, so the general rule is to season, mix and season again.
+ Mix all the ingredients until the meat has an almost sticky texture. This will help to hold the terrine together.

... Chicken, Potato and Hazelnut Terrine with Asparagus and Sweetcorn Salad / continued

I line the terrine mould with potato slices instead of bacon, as this avoids the unpleasant taste of cold bacon — or the effort of making pastry. Use bacon if you prefer. Terrines will keep in the refrigerator for 10 days, so they're perfect to make a week ahead. Serve with a salad, good crusty bread, some relish and a glass of riesling.

Ingredients / Serves 12

Terrine

butter to grease the mould

500g chicken mince

2 skinless chicken thighs

100g hazelnuts, chopped

2 cloves garlic, chopped

1 tbsp fresh thyme leaves

zest of 1 lemon

2 eggs

1 cup cream

1½ level tsp salt

1 tsp freshly ground black pepper

4 large potatoes, peeled and thinly sliced

Asparagus and Sweetcorn Salad

2 bunches asparagus, trimmed and peeled

2 cups fresh corn kernels

4 tbsp lemon-infused olive oil

juice of 1 lemon

6 basil leaves, chopped

6 stalks of chervil leaves, chopped

salt and freshly ground black pepper

Method

To make the terrine, preheat the oven to 180°C. Lightly butter a 25-centimetre long by seven-centimetre deep terrine, or loaf pan. Place the chicken mince in a large mixing bowl. Chop the chicken thighs into two-centimetre pieces and add to the bowl with the nuts, garlic, thyme and zest. Mix well. In a separate bowl, beat the eggs and cream and gently stir into the chicken mixture. Season with salt and pepper, then refrigerate.

Line the terrine with the potato slices. Start with the base, then work around the perimeter of the mould, making sure that the slices overlap slightly and that they overhang the top of the terrine so that they can be folded back over the chicken mix. Keep any extra slices to one side. Place one-third of the chicken mixture in the mould and cover with a single layer of potatoes. Repeat the process with another third of the remaining chicken mixture and more potato. Cover with the remaining mixture and fold the overhanging potatoes over the top to form a lid.

Press the terrine down lightly with your fingers to expel any air. Cover the terrine dish with a lid and place it in a deep roasting dish. Fill the dish with hot tap water until it reaches three-quarters of the way up the terrine dish. Place the dish in the oven and bake for one hour. Do not worry about any excess butter or fat that may bubble out from under the lid.

Remove the terrine from the oven and leave to cool on the bench for 30 minutes. Then place the dish on a shallow tray, remove the lid and cover the surface of the terrine with a board or something flat that fits inside the terrine. Weigh it down with something heavy, such as a brick. The juices may spill over the lip of the terrine, which is why it needs to be in a shallow tray. Cover with plastic wrap and refrigerate overnight.

To make the salad, bring a large pot of well-salted water to the boil. Drop the asparagus into the water and cook for three minutes. Carefully remove them to a colander and refresh under cold running water. Add the corn kernels to the pot and bring it back to the boil. Cook the corn for one minute. Drain, then refresh under cold running water. Pat the corn and asparagus dry in a tea towel and place in a bowl. Drizzle with the oil and lemon juice. Add the herbs and toss lightly. Season with salt and pepper.

To Serve
Turn the terrine out onto a board or platter and slice thickly. Pile the salad onto the platter next to the terrine.

B'stilla —

While researching Moroccan food for a friend's birthday lunch, I came across the North African pigeon pie called b'stilla, also known as pastilla. Both are pronounced 'pasti-ya'. The pie, which can also be made with chicken or duck, is a sweet yet slightly salty and fragrant mix of meat, spices and a crunchy layer of buttered almonds in crisp sheets of filo pastry. The recipe is fairly involved, but time can be saved by making the filling a day ahead.

  For the birthday lunch, we made individual pies, but you could make a larger one on a shallow pizza tray. With their surprise combination of textures and tastes, the b'stillas were a perfect picnic food for the guests, who sat outside on rugs and under the shade of umbrellas.

  Follow the b'stilla with slices of the moist orange cake on page 247 and a salad of orange slices splashed with orange-flower water.

Ingredients / Makes 4 pies

Filling

1 tbsp grapeseed oil
4 duck legs
salt and freshly ground black pepper
1 small onion, finely diced
1 cup white wine
a pinch of saffron threads
1 litre chicken stock
1 green apple, finely chopped

Savoury Custard

4 eggs
1 cup reduced cooking liquor

Nut Mix

60g unsalted butter
100g slivered almonds
1 tsp cinnamon
3 tbsp icing sugar
16–20 sheets filo pastry
100g unsalted butter, melted
icing sugar for dusting
cinnamon for dusting

Method

To prepare the filling, preheat the oven to 180°C. Heat the oil in a large frying pan. Brown the duck legs in the oil, then season lightly with salt and pepper. Render out some of the duck fat. Lower the heat, then add the onion. Cook until soft but without colour, then add the wine and simmer for two minutes. Add the saffron and stock. Pour all the contents into a large casserole dish, cover with a lid or tinfoil and bake in the oven for 1½ hours. Remove the duck from the dish and set aside. Pour the contents of the casserole into the frying pan and return to the heat. Continue cooking until the liquid has reduced to about a cup. Cool, then remove the skin from the duck and chop finely. Shred the meat and combine with the skin and apple.

To make the custard, bring a saucepan of water to a gentle simmer. In a bowl that fits over the pot, making sure the water is not in contact with the bottom of the bowl, whisk the eggs and liquor together. Stir constantly until thickened, then remove from the heat to cool. Fold the custard through the duck meat mixture and season with salt and pepper.

For the nut mix, melt the butter in a small frying pan. Add the almonds and fry slowly until golden, then transfer them with the butter to a small dish and place in the refrigerator to set. Once hardened, break the mixture into pieces. Put the pieces into a food processor and pulse until it has a coarse texture. Add the cinnamon and icing sugar. Transfer to a small bowl.

To assemble, spread four sheets of filo on the kitchen bench and brush each with the melted butter before layering them in a stack. Using a sharp knife, and a saucer as a guide, cut the pastry into circles through all the layers. Spread a spoonful of the nut mixture in a four-centimetre circle in the centre of the pastry, then top with a large spoonful of duck mixture. Fold the pastry up, pleating the sides. Twist the pleats at the top and turn the pastry over. The pastries can be made to this point two to three days ahead, or even frozen (defrost before use).

To cook, preheat the oven to 180°C. Brush the pastries with melted butter and bake for 15 minutes until puffed and golden. Remove from the oven and dust with icing sugar and cinnamon.

Seafood Cassoulet —

One of the staple ingredients in my pantry is canned, cooked white beans — the generic term for great northern, cannellini, coco blanc, haricot and lima beans.

With their smooth texture and lingering buttery and nutty flavours, white beans are an ideal and inexpensive filler for simple dishes. Although the beans are perfect to serve with grilled meats, I also like to use them in dishes that combine meat and seafood, as this variation on the French classic cassoulet demonstrates. The word cassoulet refers to the name of the dish it is cooked in — the cassole — but I use an oval ovenproof dish.

Serve the cassoulet straight from the cooking dish, with the shellfish and spicy chorizo sausage bubbling away under a golden, aromatic crust of breadcrumbs.

Ingredients / Serves 6

100ml white wine

400g seafood, such as prawns, oysters, mussels, clams and fish

200g unsalted butter

1 tsp chopped garlic

¼ leek, finely chopped

½ onion, finely chopped

½ carrot, peeled and finely chopped

100g bacon

150g chorizo sausage

400g can white beans, drained

1 medium potato, peeled and diced

2 tomatoes, squeezed to remove the seeds, and chopped

½ cup breadcrumbs

4 tbsp chopped chives to garnish

Method

Preheat the oven to 180°C. Put the wine and any shellfish into a saucepan and heat until they open. Remove the shellfish, reserving the juices (this will be the shellfish stock). Remove the meat from the shells and set aside. Melt the butter in a deep saucepan, then add the garlic, leek and onion. Cook until soft and golden brown, then add the carrot and cook until it looks shiny and soft. Add the bacon and chorizo and cook until fragrant. Add the beans, potato and tomatoes and enough shellfish stock to just cover the beans. Bring to a simmer then cook for 10 minutes before adding the herbs. Transfer the contents to a deep casserole dish. Add the shellfish and fish, pushing them well down into the beans. Sprinkle the surface of the cassoulet with the breadcrumbs and place the dish in the oven. Cook for about 20 minutes or until the crust is golden and the liquid has reduced. Serve immediately, sprinkled with chopped chives and accompanied by green salad and crusty bread.

Poached Fish with Barbecued Potatoes, Spinach and Black Olive Tapenade —

These barbecued potatoes served with chive aïoli (see page 258) make a great pre-dinner snack or tossed with green beans in the tapenade to make a salad. This is an adaptable feast.

Ingredients / Serves 4

Barbecued Potatoes

4 medium Agria potatoes in their skins
1 tsp each of chopped fresh thyme, tarragon and parsley
4 tbsp unsalted butter, softened, or olive oil
salt and freshly ground black pepper

Poached Fish

2 tsp unsalted butter
1 tbsp chopped onion
800g fish fillets, eg monkfish, blue cod, groper
salt
1 cup chicken stock
1 cup water
100ml white wine
juice of 1 lemon
1kg spinach leaves, washed with stems removed

Black Olive Tapenade
Makes 2 cups

500g large black olives, pitted
2 cloves garlic
75g anchovies in oil, drained
2 tbsp capers, drained
100ml olive oil
pepper

Method

To prepare the potatoes, preheat the oven to 180°C. Wrap the potatoes in tinfoil and bake for 40 minutes. They should not be fully cooked when you remove them. Allow to cool in the tinfoil. (This may be done several days ahead.) Heat the barbecue. Rub the skins from the potatoes, or peel carefully. Slice the potatoes into one-centimetre-thick rounds. Mix the herbs and butter or oil and brush the potato slices. Place the slices on the grill and season with salt and pepper. Cook until golden brown. Depending on the heat of the barbecue, this should take no more than five minutes.

To prepare the fish, melt the butter in a deep frying pan. Add the onion and cook until soft but without colour. Place the fish on top, season lightly with salt, then add the stock, water, wine and lemon juice. Cut a piece of greaseproof paper to fit over the pan and bring the liquid to a gentle simmer. Cook for five minutes, then remove the fish from the pan, drain well and keep warm. Reduce the liquid in the pan to half a cup and add the spinach. Wilt the leaves in the stock for no more than two minutes then drain well.

To make the tapenade, blend the ingredients in a food processor until a smooth paste forms. Transfer into small jars and store in the refrigerator. It will keep in the refrigerator for months.

To Serve
Place the barbecued potatoes on a serving platter and cover with spinach. Lay the fish on top and spoon the tapenade over each piece.

Grilled Fish and Fresh Peas with Prawn Mashed Potatoes —

Summer dining liberates us from napkins, table settings, polished glasses and matching cutlery, although I still use candles at dinner. What we cook is suggested by thoughts of smoky grills, platters of food placed in the centre of the table and meals not planned.

I usually start by thinking of grilling fish, and go from there — and I avoid dishes that involve the oven.

Ingredients / Serves 4

Prawn Mashed Potatoes

1 litre hot water (from the tap)
500g Agria potatoes, peeled and cut into 1-cm slices
120ml cream or milk
120g unsalted butter
salt
300g prawn cutlets, cooked and roughly chopped
½ bunch spring onions, green part finely sliced

Fish and Peas

800g firm white-fleshed fish fillets (such as snapper, groper, tarakihi)
2 tbsp unsalted butter, melted
salt
1 lemon
2 cups fresh peas, shelled
2 tbsp unsalted butter

Method

To prepare the mashed potatoes, put the water and potatoes into a saucepan. Cook 45–50 minutes until tender and drain. Do not run the potatoes under cold water. Instead, return them to the saucepan over a low heat. Shake the pan to allow as much moisture as possible to evaporate. Put the potatoes through a ricer or a mouli or beat with a wooden spoon until smooth. Heat the cream or milk, then add the butter, stirring until melted. Beat into the potatoes and season with salt. Stir in the prawns and spring onion. Set aside in a warm place. Alternatively, refrigerate until required and reheat over a gentle heat with a little bit of hot milk.

To cook the fish, heat the grill or barbecue. Brush the fish with the melted butter and cook for about three minutes. Turn the fish, season with salt and cook for another three minutes, depending on the thickness. Remove the fish to a plate, squeeze lemon juice over it and keep it warm.

Bring a pot of salted water to the boil. Cook the peas for three minutes, then drain and toss them with the second measure of butter.

To Serve

Place a mound of mashed potato on each plate and top with a piece of fish. Serve the peas on the side.

Grilled Salmon and Soba Noodle Salad with Rock Sugar Dressing —

This simple recipe uses rock sugar, also known as yellow sugar, which is available from most Asian supermarkets.

Ingredients / Serves 4

Salad

4 heads bok choy, rinsed
270g packet soba noodles
1 tsp sesame oil
1 tsp sesame seeds
2 tsp olive oil
700g piece of salmon fillet, cut into 4 pieces
sea salt

Rock Sugar Dressing
Makes 1 cup

100g rock or yellow sugar
50ml white vinegar
15g fresh root ginger, grated
50ml mirin (sweet sake)
2 tsp soy sauce
3 tbsp lime juice
1 small onion, finely chopped
2 cloves garlic, finely chopped
2 stalks spring onions, finely sliced
2 tbsp chopped coriander leaves

Method

To make the salad, bring a large saucepan of salted water to the boil. Cut the bok choy heads in half, add to the saucepan and cook for three minutes. Using a sieve or kitchen tongs, remove the bok choy from the pan to a bowl lined with a damp tea towel to keep warm. Return the water to the boil, add the noodles and cook them for four minutes. Drain. Toss the hot noodles in the sesame oil and seeds, then set them aside to keep warm while you cook the salmon.

Heat a frying pan and rub some olive oil on to the salmon pieces. Place the salmon in the hot pan and cook for three minutes. Turn the pieces over, sprinkle the cooked side with sea salt and cook for a further three minutes.

To make the dressing, crush the rock sugar. Combine it with the vinegar in a small saucepan over a low heat and stir until dissolved. Cool. Mix in the remaining ingredients. Transfer to a jar and refrigerate until required. It will keep in the refrigerator for three months.

To Serve

Transfer the salmon to four serving plates. Toss the noodles in the dressing and place a pile of them next to each piece of salmon. Top the noodles with the warm bok choy and serve immediately.

Grilled Tuna with Scarlet Runners, Prosciutto and Potato Salad with Caper Dressing —

Simple, light and quick to make, this refreshing salad is perfect for lunch or dinner. The dressing can be made while the potatoes and beans cook. It would also be great made with groper, snapper or blue cod instead of tuna.

Ingredients / Serves 4

4 x 100g pieces fresh tuna

2 tbsp olive oil

sea salt

juice of 1 lemon

2 cups cooked potatoes

2 tbsp chopped chives

1 tbsp virgin olive oil

salt and freshly ground black pepper

4–6 slices of prosciutto

300g scarlet runner beans, trimmed and cooked

Caper Dressing

2 tbsp capers

1 tbsp red wine vinegar

1 clove garlic, finely chopped

freshly ground black pepper

zest of 1 lemon

½ tsp of chopped fresh thyme leaves

½ cup virgin olive oil

Method

Heat a frying pan until hot. Brush the tuna with oil and carefully place the pieces in the hot pan. Sear for one minute on each side. Remove the tuna from the pan and season with sea salt and a squeeze of lemon juice.

Toss the warm potatoes with the chives, the second measure of olive oil, and season with salt and pepper. Cut the prosciutto into wide strips and add to the potatoes.

To make the dressing, soak the capers in a bowl of cold water for 30 minutes. Drain and finely chop, then place them in a small bowl. Stir in the vinegar, garlic, pepper, lemon zest and thyme leaves. Mix in the olive oil until it forms a smoothish paste.

To Serve

Slice the warm beans and arrange with the potato salad on individual plates. Slice the tuna steaks in half and place on top of the salad. Drizzle with caper dressing.

Grilled Fish with Roast Kumara Purée and Red Wine and Mushroom Ragoût —

I enjoy the play of flavours in this dish, with a rich and surprising earthiness coming from the mushrooms. Don't let anyone tell you that red wine does not go with fish — it can handle bold flavours, and be treated robustly. Blue cod is wonderful with mushrooms because of its slight mineral taste, but if you can't get it use monkfish.

Ingredients / Serves 4

Kumara Purée

500g kumara

olive oil for roasting

50g unsalted butter

salt and freshly ground black pepper

Red Wine and Mushroom Ragoût

50g unsalted butter

2 shallots, thinly sliced

8 portobello mushrooms, thinly sliced

1 sprig fresh thyme

1 bay leaf

250ml red wine

250ml chicken stock

Fish

800g firm white-fleshed fish fillets

2 tbsp unsalted butter, melted

salt

juice of 1 lemon

Method

To make the purée, preheat the oven to 180°C. Scrub the kumara clean, coat in the oil and bake in the oven until tender, for about 30 minutes. Remove from the oven and when cool enough to handle peel off the skin. Purée the remaining flesh of the kumara in a food processor until smooth, adding the butter. Season and set to one side, keeping warm.

To make the ragoût, heat the butter in a deep saucepan and when it begins to foam add the shallots. Cook for three minutes, then add the mushrooms and cook for a further eight minutes until the mushrooms are nice and soft. Add the herbs and wine, and simmer for five minutes. Pour in the stock and bring back to a gentle simmer, reducing by half until the sauce becomes lovely and syrupy.

To cook the fish, preheat the grill. Place the portions of fish on a shallow baking sheet and brush with the melted butter. Put the fish under the grill and cook for three minutes, Turn the fish, season with salt and cook for another three minutes depending on the thickness of the fillet. Remove the fish to a plate, add the lemon juice and keep it warm.

To Serve

Place the fish on the kumara purée and spoon the ragoût over the top.

Fish Braised with Tomatoes, Mussels and Cockles —

Based loosely on something Moroccan, this is a delightful fish stew with terrific base flavours that carry through to make a blockbuster of a dish. Serve with some fabulous crusty bread, sliced and splashed with olive oil.

Ingredients / Serves 6

6 tbsp olive oil

3 anchovy fillets

1 red onion

2 garlic cloves

1 sprig fresh rosemary

2 bay leaves

2 red capsicums, seeded and sliced

330g can whole peeled tomatoes

½ cup white wine

½ cup chicken stock

a pinch of saffron

150g toasted ground almonds

salt and freshly ground black pepper

400g firm white fish

300g mussels

300g cockles

Method

Heat the oil in a wide frying pan over a medium heat and add the anchovies and chopped onion. Cook for about 15 minutes until pale gold, and the anchovies have become a paste. Add the garlic, rosemary, bay leaves and red capsicums. Cook for 10 minutes until the peppers are lovely and soft. Add the tomatoes, breaking them up with a wooden spoon as you simmer them for 10 minutes. Add the wine, and chicken stock with saffron (infuse the saffron in the chicken stock before adding it). Add the almonds to thicken the sauce and season with salt and freshly ground black pepper. Add the fish, mussels and cockles, then cover with a lid and cook for five minutes. Serve direct from the pan.

Barbecued Lamb Rump with Charred Vegetables and Anchovy Butter —

This is the kind of dish that needs to be served on a platter for friends and family to help themselves. It's full of the sort of natural flavours that love being in each other's company.

Ingredients / Serves 6

3 lamb rumps
salt and freshly ground black pepper
100ml olive oil
juice of 1 lemon
1 large aubergine, sliced in rings
2 red capsicums, deseeded and sliced
2 zucchini, sliced diagonally
2 red onions, sliced into eighths
2 small fennel bulbs, sliced
olive oil
6 tbsp anchovy butter (see page 257)
lemon wedges to garnish

Method

Heat the barbecue. Trim the fat off the lamb and season with the salt and pepper. Rub the lamb with oil and place on the grill. After a few minutes turn the rumps 45° and continue to cook until well browned and then turn over again. The lamb will need about 15 minutes total cooking time, but make sure it doesn't burn. Season occasionally with salt and pepper. Once the meat is cooked, remove it to a plate to rest and add the lemon juice.

Put all the prepared vegetables into a bowl, season with salt and pepper and toss with a liberal amount of olive oil — be reasonably generous, as the aubergine soaks it up. Put the vegetables on the grill and as each one cooks, remove it to another bowl. Season again, if required, and add more oil if the vegetables need moistening.

To Serve

Arrange the vegetables on a platter. Slice each rump into thirds and place on top of the vegetables. Soften the anchovy butter and spoon over. Garnish with lemon wedges.

Grilled Lamb Rump with Chorizo Sausage, Chickpeas and Mushrooms and Apple and Onion Salad —

Lamb rumps are quick and easy roast dinners, the sweet meat a marvellous companion to other flavours. The lamb rump is considered to be a secondary cut of meat, but it becomes sophisticated, balanced and elegant when served with the aromatic and earthy chickpeas. I used canned chickpeas for the sauté, rinsing them first. The vague smoky flavours of the chorizo sausage wrap the mushrooms like a warm blanket, and the salad provides a simple cleansing contrast.

Ingredients / Serves 4

Lamb, Chorizo, Chickpeas and Mushrooms

2 tbsp vegetable oil

4 lamb rumps, trimmed of any excess fat

salt and freshly ground black pepper

2 tbsp olive oil

2 cloves garlic, peeled and chopped

6 Portobello mushrooms, sliced ½ cm thick

150g chorizo sausage, sliced on an angle

200g cooked chickpeas, washed and drained

juice of 1 lemon

1 tbsp chopped parsley

Apple and Onion Salad

1 medium red onion, thinly sliced

2 apples, thinly sliced

3 tbsp cider vinegar

2 tsp sugar

1 tsp Worcestershire sauce

salt and freshly ground black pepper

100ml olive oil

½ cup crème fraîche

2 tbsp chopped fennel

Method

Preheat the oven to 180°C. Heat the vegetable oil in a frying pan large enough to hold the rumps (and that you can later place in the oven). Place the rumps into the hot oil and brown on all sides, seasoning, as you turn the pieces, with salt and pepper. Put the frying pan in the oven for 12–15 minutes until the lamb is tender. Remove the lamb from the oven and keep warm. Place the pan the lamb was cooked in over a medium heat on the stovetop, heating the olive oil. Sauté the garlic until golden and then add the mushrooms and the chorizo sausage. Cook until the mushrooms soften and the chorizo become fragrant. Stir in the chickpeas and warm through, adding the lemon juice and the chopped parsley. Season with more salt and pepper.

To make the salad, mix the onion and apple together in a small bowl. In a separate bowl mix the vinegar with the sugar, Worcestershire sauce, and salt and pepper. Whisk in the olive oil and crème fraîche and stir in the fennel. Gently toss the dressing through the apples and onions.

To Serve

Slice the lamb rumps and place on individual serving plates and divide the chickpea mixture between them. Place spoonfuls of the salad next to the lamb.

Slow-cooked Beef Cheeks, Smoked Eel, Young Carrots and Celeriac Purée —

I sometimes think the phrase 'slow-cooked' is a much better description for braising, because it evokes images of extremely tender and tasty meat. Richly satisfying, slow cooking is true cooking and it shows the skill of a cook to full advantage.

Visit your local butcher to obtain the beef cheeks for this recipe — and even if he has to get them in for you, it will still be well worth the effort. If cheeks are unavailable, this recipe works just as well with oxtail, brisket, shanks or shoulder. You want meat with plenty of connective tissue that will dissolve into gelatine, as this is what makes slow-cooked meat so succulently moist and fork-tender. Always sear the meat first to caramelise it. This adds complex roasted flavours to the dish and gives the stock a deeper colour. (Contrary to popular opinion, searing does not seal in any juices.)

In this dish, I use the smoked eel like bacon to impart a beautiful smoky aroma — it even looks like bacon. The vegetables that are cooked with the beef may also be served with the meal, but as they have contributed all their flavour to the stock, it's better to cook some fresh vegetables just before serving. As with the carrots, you can add a little spice — in this case cardamom, which brings more fragrance than taste to the dish. The beef cheeks can be done two to three days in advance, and then reheated with the sauce and vegetables in a covered pan in an oven heated to 160°C. When cold, the cheeks resemble small rocks, but they are easy to slice. Once reheated, they quickly become soft and tender.

Ingredients / Serves 6

6 whole beef cheeks

30ml olive oil

salt and freshly ground black pepper

1 litre red wine

4 cloves garlic

8 shallots

1 medium onion, sliced

4 medium carrots, peeled and cut into 1-cm-thick slices

6 star anise

4 sprigs fresh thyme

2 bay leaves

1 tsp black peppercorns

400ml beef stock

200g button mushrooms

200g smoked eel, cut into 1-cm cubes

optional: 18 young carrots, peeled to serve

2 tbsp unsalted butter

1 tbsp cardamom pods

Celeriac Purée

1 large celeriac, peeled and diced

2 bay leaves

600ml milk

1 tbsp unsalted butter

salt and freshly ground black pepper

fresh thyme for garnish

Method

Heat the oven to 160°C. Trim the excess fat from the beef cheeks. Heat the oil in a heavy frying pan and brown the cheeks on all sides until nicely caramelised. Lift them from the pan and drain on absorbent paper. Season generously with salt and pepper. Pour the wine into the frying pan and bring it to a rapid boil for five minutes. Place the garlic, shallots, onion and carrots in a roasting dish suitable for stovetop use, then arrange the cheeks on top.

Tie the star anise, thyme, bay leaves and peppercorns in a piece of muslin and add to the dish. Pour in the wine and stock. Bring the contents of the pan to a simmer on top of the stove and cover with a piece of baking paper. Cover this with tinfoil. Place in the oven and cook for two hours. Remove the dish from the oven and carefully fold back the foil and paper. Add the mushrooms, then replace the cover and return the dish to the oven for another 45 minutes.

Remove the cheeks from the cooking stock while they are hot — do this carefully as they will be very delicate. Allow them to cool, then slice thickly. Strain the stock and you can either discard the vegetables or chop into smaller pieces to be served with the meat. Discard the bag of herbs and spices. Pour the cooking stock into a clean saucepan and simmer until it has reduced by half to make a rich sauce. Add the smoked eel and the cheeks and the cooking vegetables, if using.

To make the purée, place the celeriac, bay leaves and enough milk to cover the celeriac in a saucepan. Bring to a simmer and cook for 30 minutes until the celeriac is tender. Strain the celeriac, reserving the milk but discarding the bay leaves. Put the celeriac into a food processor and blend until smooth, adding the butter and just enough milk to make a velvety purée. Season lightly.

Place the carrots in a frying pan with the butter and the cardamom pods and cook for five minutes or until tender.

To Serve
Place a spoon of purée on each plate and top with spoonfuls of the cheeks, eel and sauce. Arrange three carrots around each plate and sprinkle with fresh thyme if desired.

Beef à la Ficelle —

This poached fillet of beef with aromatic vegetables is prepared by dangling the beef as the French do à la ficelle — on a string — into a deep pot of stock.

Ingredients / Serves 6

6 x 180g beef fillet steaks

2 tbsp olive oil

salt and pepper

1 onion, sliced

2 medium carrots, peeled and cut into 1-cm dice

6 baby beetroot, peeled

2 medium potatoes, peeled and balled using a melon baller

12 baby turnips, peeled

1 litre beef stock

1 litre chicken stock

1 bay leaf

1 sprig fresh thyme

2 cloves garlic

12 spears asparagus, cooked

sea salt

2 tbsp horseradish cream

Method

Tie each steak with butcher's twine, making sure to leave one long end. The twine will help to retain the shape of the meat as well as giving you a means to lift it from the stock. Heat the oil in a frying pan and quickly sear the beef on all sides. Season with salt and pepper. Remove the beef to a deep pot and hang the long ends of twine over the sides. (I tie the ends to the pot handles.)

Add the onion, carrots, beetroot, potatoes and turnips to the pot. Add the stocks and bring to a gentle simmer, then add the herbs and garlic. Cook the steaks for 12 minutes (for medium rare) from the time the broth starts to simmer. Lift the steaks out of the stock, remove the twine and cover while they rest for 10 minutes.

To Serve

Lift the vegetables out of the stock and divide them between six bowls. Divide the cooked asparagus between the bowls (the hot stock will warm the spears through). Ladle the stock over the vegetables. Cut each steak in half and place the pieces in the centre. Sprinkle with sea salt and serve with horseradish cream.

Grilled Steak with Rosemary and Garlic Fried Potatoes, Green Beans and Reduced Pan Juices —

This is one of those simple dishes that can be achieved any night of the week. The potatoes themselves are addictive ... I have one guest who regularly asks for an extra dish of them on the side.

Ingredients / Serves 4

4 medium Agria potatoes, washed but not peeled

3 tbsp olive oil

4 x 180g beef steaks

2 tbsp unsalted butter

salt and freshly ground black pepper

125ml red wine

300ml olive oil

8 cloves garlic, unpeeled and lightly crushed

2 sprigs fresh rosemary, leaves picked off the stem

400g green beans, shredded

Method

Bring the potatoes to the boil in a large pot of water. Cook for about 30 minutes until the skins start to peel and the centre feels tender when tested with a sharp knife. Drain the potatoes and let them cool. Do not run them under cold water or they will go soggy! When they're cool enough to handle, peel and dice into three-centimetre cubes. The potatoes can be done days ahead and kept in the refrigerator.

Heat two tablespoons of the oil in a frying pan and fry the steaks until they are browned. Add the butter, then turn the steaks over and finish cooking to suit your preference, basting with the juices as they cook. Season with salt and pepper. Remove the steaks to a plate to rest and keep them warm. Pour the wine into the pan and bring to the boil. Stir to loosen any bits of meat that may have stuck to the pan and reduce the juices by half — about three minutes.

In a deep frying pan heat the 300ml of olive oil. Add the potatoes and cook for five minutes or until they begin to develop a golden crust. Add the garlic and rosemary and cook for a further five minutes. Carefully lift the potatoes out and place on paper towels, and season with salt and pepper.

Bring a pot of salted water to the boil and blanch the beans for two minutes. Drain and toss them in a bowl with the remaining tablespoon of oil and some salt and pepper.

To Serve

Place the steaks onto individual serving plates and spoon over the reduced pan juices. Pile the potatoes and beans on the side.

Pan-fried Fillet Steak with Potato Gnocchi, Prosciutto and Brussel Sprouts and Grain Mustard Sauce —

A properly cooked steak, with a crisp layer of a generous seasoning of salt and pepper, served with potato gnocchi speaks for itself; it feels masculine, yet has a subtle sensuality about it with the creamy grain mustard sauce. Brussel sprouts suffer from a sad reputation; but when cooked properly can be tempting.

Ingredients / Serves 4

2 tbsp olive oil
4 x 180–200g fillet steaks
2 tbsp unsalted butter
salt and freshly ground black pepper
½ cup dry sherry
½ cup beef stock
1 tbsp grain mustard
50ml cream
juice of 1 lemon
400g store-bought potato gnocchi, cooked
300g Brussel sprouts, trimmed and quartered
80g unsalted butter
1 medium onion, thinly sliced
6 thin slices of Prosciutto, cut into thin ribbons

Method

To cook the steak, heat the olive oil in a frying pan and put in the steaks. Fry on one side to a lovely brown colour. Add the butter and turn the steaks over. Season with salt and pepper, and baste the steaks with the juices as you cook them to your preferred state of doneness. Remove the steaks to plate to rest and keep warm. Pour the sherry into the frying pan and return to the heat. Simmer for two minutes and scrape up any sticky bits that have stuck to the pan, add the beef stock and simmer for a further three minutes, then stir in the grain mustard and cream. Pour in any juices from the steak that may have accumulated on the resting plate, bring the liquid back to a simmer, and add the lemon juice and season.

To cook the gnocchi and sprouts, bring a large pot of salted water to a vicious boil, and briefly cook the gnocchi, removing them from the water as they float to the top. When all the gnocchi are cooked drop the Brussels sprouts into the same water and boil for about three minutes. Drain the sprouts and set to one side. Heat a frying pan on a high heat, add the butter and onion and cook until translucent. Then add the gnocchi, prosciutto and the cooked sprouts. Sauté until the sprouts begin to take on a little colour and become tender. Season with salt and pepper.

To Serve

Arrange the sprout mixture on individual serving plates. Place a steak alongside each pile and spoon over the sauce.

Braised Short Ribs, Green Olives and Currants with Roast Parsnips and Spinach —

The short ribs are a cut from just behind the chuck, but if you cannot get your butcher to provide them for you — surprisingly many butchers do not know what they are — then by all means use brisket. Make this ahead of time if you wish, and reheat it when you want. It improves greatly after a few days kept in the refrigerator.

Ingredients / Serves 6-8

750ml red wine
3 tbsp brandy
2 tbsp vegetable oil
1.5 kg beef short ribs, bone in and trimmed
salt and freshly ground black pepper
1 medium onion, finely chopped
1 medium carrot, peeled and finely chopped
2 cloves garlic
2 sprigs fresh thyme
2 bay leaves
1 tsp black peppercorns
400ml beef stock
½ cup green olives, washed
½ cup currants
1 cup of cooked spinach leaves

Roast Parsnips

3–4 parsnips, peeled and halved lengthways
olive oil
4 cloves garlic, unpeeled but crushed
salt and freshly ground black pepper

Method

Preheat the oven to 180°C. Pour the wine and brandy into a saucepan and boil for two minutes to evaporate the alcohol, without setting fire to the contents, and remove from the heat. Place a large frying pan (that you can put in the oven) or casserole dish over a high heat. Add the oil and brown the short ribs until the meat is nicely caramelised. Drain away any excess oil. Season the ribs all over with the salt and pepper. Remove the ribs to a plate, and add the vegetables, garlic, peppercorns and herbs to the pan and brown lightly for five minutes or so. Then return the ribs to the pan along with the wine, brandy and stock. If there is not enough stock to cover the ribs add some water and bring to a boil on top of the stove. Cover with a piece of baking paper and then a lid or tinfoil. Place the pan into the oven and let it gently simmer away for 2 ½ hours, until the ribs are tender enough to pierce with a fork. Carefully remove the ribs from the stock and keep them warm on a serving platter. Strain the stock into a clean saucepan and add the olives and currants. Bring the stock back to a simmer on top of the stove until it is reduced by half and has thickened slightly, then season.

To roast the parsnips, toss with the olive oil, garlic and a little salt and pepper and roast for 45 minutes, until tender and lightly browned.

To Serve

Pour the sauce with the olives and currants over the ribs and serve with the spinach and parsnips.

Slow-cooked Pork Belly with Aromatic Spices and Plums —

The versatile plum is ideal for salads and savoury dishes. The pork can be cooked ahead and left in the fridge for a few days, then sliced and fried in a little oil before being finished in a hot oven for 12 minutes. The advantage of doing this is that the fat will become satisfyingly crisp. Reheat the sauce separately.

Ingredients / Serves 6

2kg pork belly, ribs removed

1 litre chicken stock

1 cinnamon quill

2 star anise

1 tsp cloves

3-cm piece of root ginger, peeled

3 cloves garlic

100ml light soy sauce

2 tbsp soft brown sugar

6 black Doris plums, halved and pitted

salt and freshly ground black pepper

Method

Place the pork in a deep pot and pour in enough stock to cover the meat, topping up with water if necessary. Add the spices, ginger and garlic. Cover and bring to a gentle simmer, then cook for two hours until the meat is tender. Carefully remove the meat to a tray and keep it warm. Add the soy sauce, sugar and plums to the liquid and cook for about 15 minutes until it is dark, fragrant and reduced by half.

To Serve

Slice the meat into six pieces and arrange on individual plates. Season lightly with salt and pepper. Spoon the sauce over each serving and garnish with plums and some of the spices. Serve with a bowl of steamed rice and steamed greens on the side.

Bolognese-style Pork Loin Braised in Milk —

The pork loin in this recipe cooks slowly in milk that eventually reduces to form small clusters of deliciously caramelised nut-brown solids. Keep the fat on the loin — it will render during cooking, keeping the loin moist as it does so. The fat is easily poured off and discarded at the end. The recipe is based on one from *The Essentials of Italian Cooking* by Marcella Hazan.

Ingredients / Serves 8

2 tbsp vegetable oil
1 tbsp butter
1.2kg loin of pork, ribs removed
salt and freshly ground black pepper
600ml milk (more, if required)

Method

Heat the oil in a casserole pan large enough to contain the pork loin. Add the butter and when it foams add the meat fat-side down. Brown the meat on all sides, lowering the heat if the butter browns too much. Season with salt and pepper, then slowly add 250ml of the milk, ensuring that it does not boil over. Allow the milk to come to a brisk simmer for 20–30 seconds, then lower the heat and cover the pan with a lid, leaving it slightly askew to allow steam to escape. Cook at a lazy simmer for one hour until the milk has thickened to a nut-brown sauce. When it reaches this stage, add another 250ml of milk, simmer for 10 minutes and cover again, this time with the lid on tightly.

After 30 more minutes, set the lid askew again and simmer until there is almost no liquid left in the pot. Add the remaining milk and cook until all the milk has coagulated into small nut-brown clusters. The whole process should take 2 ½ to three hours. If all the milk evaporates before the meat is fully cooked, add another 100ml or so.

Transfer the meat to a cutting board and pour off the fat, leaving behind the milk clusters. Add two or three tbsps of water to the pot and bring to the boil, scraping all the cooked residues from the bottom and sides of the pot.

To Serve

Slice the pork and spoon the milky juices over it. Serve immediately, accompanied by green beans, broccoli or spinach.

Grilled Pork Chops with White Beans, Fennel and Spicy Sausage —

It may seem unusual to eat a pork-based sausage with a pork chop, but it actually works. Based on an Italian recipe, the white beans with the fennel and sausage also go well with grilled lamb or roast chicken. The best part of this dish is that you are eating it within 30 minutes of cooking it.

Ingredients / Serves 4

100g unsalted butter
4 pork chops
salt and freshly ground black pepper
2 cloves garlic, peeled and crushed
150g spicy pork sausage, finely diced
2 tbsp dry sherry
200g white beans, cooked
2 fennel bulbs, thinly sliced
300ml cream

Method

Melt half the butter in a shallow frying pan until it begins foaming, then add the chops. Cook until golden brown, about four minutes, turn them over, season and cook for another four to six minutes or until the juices run clear. Remove the chops from the pan and keep them warm. Add the remaining butter to the pan and cook the garlic until golden brown. Add the spicy sausage and cook until fragrant, about two minutes, then pour in the sherry and cook for one minute. Stir in the white beans, fennel and cream, and simmer until reduced by half and the fennel is just cooked. Taste the sauce, and season with salt and pepper.

To Serve

Divide the bean mixture among individual plates and place a pork chop on top.

Desserts & Baking.

Making desserts always seems to invoke more angst than is really necessary, yet they are the dishes most likely to elicit appreciative 'oohs' and 'aahs' from your guests. Believe me, I understand this anxiety — pastry and I used to dislike each other intensely until I decided that it was really mind over butter and flour, and I determined to conquer it.

In summer, a piece of fresh fruit is all you really need for dessert. A ripe peach is full of flavour; a bowl of cherries, chilled on ice, is irresistible; and a thick slice of watermelon is the best thirst-quencher ever. Occasionally you might want to stretch yourself and cook something a little more dramatic: poach some overripe berries and serve with a white chocolate mousse; or grill some peaches and serve with crème fraîche, for instance.

In autumn and through into winter come the apples, pears, feijoas, tamarillos and kiwifruit. These are transformed by a little effort — a simple apple tart with a tender, golden crust, or some poached tamarillos to accompany a rich rice pudding. The following recipes require some effort — not much, I promise — but if you make the time family and friends will adore you for it.

This Section

Baked Meringues with
Poached Cherries and
Toffee Popcorn **194**

Basil Panna Cotta with
Berry Coulis **197**

Orange and Cardamom
Crème Brûlée **199**

Coffee and Anise Bavarois **202**

Raspberry Semifreddo
with Ginger Biscuits **205**

Poached Peach with
Lemon Verbena Sabayon **206**

Grilled Peaches with
Almond Biscuit, Crème
Fraîche and Mint **209**

White Chocolate Mousse
and Raspberries **211**

Chocolate Terrine with
Mandarin Sauce **213**

Chocolate Mousse **217**

Rich Rice Pudding,
Poached Tamarillos
and Marmalade **218**

Pear and Almond
Frangipane Tart **221**

Fine Apple Tart **222**

Tarte Tatin **227**

Deep Lemon Tart
with Raspberries and
Citrus Syrup **228**

Mascarpone Cream
with Berry Salad **231**

Strawberry Sponge
with Lemon Verbena
and Orange Salad **233**

Strawberry and Orange Salad,
Mascarpone Puff Pastry
and Candied Capsicums **235**

Christmas Pudding **240**

Cherry Financier **243**

Plum, Walnut Oil and
Sweet Wine Cake with
Plum Compote **244**

Orange and Almond Cake **247**

Lemon Shortbread **248**

Baked Meringues with Poached Cherries and Toffee Popcorn —

The French dessert of poached meringue known as Ile Flottante was the inspiration for this dish, but I gave it a twist with the toffeed popcorn and added the poached cherries to round out the sweetness. The delicate meringue majestically floats in a crimson-hued pool of cherry juices.

Ingredients / Serves 6

Meringues

5 egg whites	
1 cup sugar	

Poached Cherries

2 cups cherries, pitted	
1 cup water	
½ cup sugar	

Toffee Popcorn

2 tbsp water	
½ cup sugar	
1 cup cooked popcorn	

Method

To make the meringues, preheat the oven to 180°C. Lightly grease six ovenproof ramekins. Beat the egg whites and sugar until the mixture is satiny smooth and forms stiff peaks. Place spoonfuls of the meringue into the ramekins and smooth the tops. Place the ramekins in a deep roasting dish and pour in enough hot water to come halfway up the sides. Cover the roasting dish with tinfoil and bake for 30 minutes until the meringues are set. Remove the ramekins from the roasting dish and refrigerate for at least an hour. When you're ready to use them, invert the meringues onto a paper towel to absorb any excess water.

To poach the cherries, place them in a saucepan with the water and sugar and bring to a gentle simmer for two minutes. Remove the pan from the heat and allow the cherries to cool in the syrup.

To make the toffee popcorn, place the water and sugar in a small pan and cook until they form a golden caramel. Add the popcorn and gently stir. Immediately remove the pan from the heat and pour the contents onto a baking sheet lined with non-stick greaseproof paper. Allow to cool. Once it's cold enough to handle, break the popcorn into small pieces.

To Serve

Place the meringues on individual serving plates. Spoon the cherries around the meringue and sprinkle the toffee popcorn around the plate.

Basil Panna Cotta with Berry Coulis —

Panna cotta is a traditional Italian dessert made by simmering together cream, milk and sugar and mixing in some gelatine to set the mix. The domestic art of jam-making seems to be in decline, but jam-quality berries are all you need to make coulis. The combination of flavours makes this an irresistible dessert.

Ingredients / Serves 6

Panna Cotta

350ml cream

150ml milk

100g sugar

1 cup of tightly packed basil, leaves only

6 tsp powdered gelatine

1 tbsp water

Coulis

1 cup of blackberries, raspberries, strawberries or blueberries

1 cup sugar

2 cups water

juice of 1 lime

½ cup each of strawberries, raspberries, blackberries and blueberries

Method

To make the panna cotta, heat the cream, milk and sugar in a saucepan, simmer for two minutes then remove from the heat. Add the basil and allow to infuse for five minutes. Dissolve the gelatine in the water and add it to the hot cream. Return the pan to the stove and stir until the gelatine has dissolved — about two minutes. Strain the mixture into a jug and allow it to cool. Just before it begins to set, pour the custard into six lightly greased ramekins and refrigerate for four hours or preferably overnight.

To make the coulis, first wash and drain the fruit. Combine the sugar and water in a saucepan and simmer for two minutes. Set it aside to cool then add the lime juice and pour into a blender. Purée until smooth, then pass it through a sieve to remove any seeds. Allow it to cool in the refrigerator.

To Serve

Pour a little of the coulis onto each plate and gently pull the top edge of the panna cotta away from the sides of the ramekins. Invert a ramekin over each serving plate, gently shaking the panna cotta free. Serve with a bowl of mixed berries.

Orange and Cardamom Crème Brûlée —

Cream, eggs and sugar are the three key ingredients for many desserts, from crème caramel and tarts to ice-creams and brûlées. If you look at brûlée recipes, you'll see that there are spectacularly differing weights and methods for the same three ingredients; no wonder it's difficult to define.

Crème brûlée translates as 'burnt cream', which sounds a little off-putting — a shame for such a beautiful dessert. The first time I put this dish on a restaurant menu it was a disaster. Our guests thought brûlée meant one thing whereas I thought it was another. My arrogance prevailed until, after nearly two years of having brûlées sent back to the kitchen because they were either too set or too sloppy, or had been baked when they should have been set overnight or — worse still — set with gelatine, I took the dish off the menu.

Don't be intimidated by the thought of making one, though. Keep the heat low, stir continuously and watch closely for the custard to thicken and take on a glossy appearance. Do not allow the eggs to scramble or curdle during cooking.

This is the definitive recipe, but the orange and cardamom can be replaced with lime, vanilla or whatever flavour you prefer.

Ingredients / Serves 4

600ml cream

6 cardamom pods, broken, seeds removed and set aside

grated zest of 1 orange

5 egg yolks

75g caster sugar

4 tbsp caster sugar for caramelising the tops of the custards

Method

Preheat the oven to 180°C. Heat the cream with the black seeds from the cardamom pods and the orange zest. Simmer for three minutes to allow the flavours to infuse. Remove from the heat and set aside for 20 minutes. Beat together the egg yolks and the first measure of caster sugar until pale and creamy. Strain the hot cream and stir it into the yolk mixture. Return the custard to a low heat and stir it continuously with a wooden spoon until it begins to thicken, whisking quickly when it does. This should take about 10–15 minutes.

Once the custard is almost set, remove it from the heat and pour it into the four ramekins. Stand the ramekins in a baking dish with enough water to come halfway up the sides. Put the dish in the oven and bake for 20 minutes. Remove the ramekins from the oven and refrigerate for at least one hour before serving.

Sprinkle one tablespoon of sugar evenly over the top of each custard, then spray with a little water. Melt the sugar under a grill until it has caramelised to a rich golden brown. Alternatively, use a hand-held kitchen blowtorch to caramelise the sugar.

**Orange and Cardamom
Crème Brûlée**
Recipe on page 199

Coffee and Anise Bavarois —

The bavarois has an interesting combination of flavours, with hints of the exotic, and it possesses a silky and seductive texture.

Ingredients / Serves 6

3 tsp gelatine powder
600ml milk
60ml espresso coffee
3 star anise
5 egg yolks
120g sugar
300ml cream

Method

Dissolve the gelatine in a little hot water. Heat the milk with the coffee and star anise in a pan. In a bowl, whisk together the egg yolks and sugar, then pour in the hot milk. Return the mixture to the pan, place over a gentle heat and cook until it has thickened like custard.

Stir in the gelatine. Pass the mixture through a sieve into a chilled bowl. Refrigerate, stirring occasionally, until the mixture starts to set — approximately 10 minutes.

Lightly whip the cream and carefully but quickly fold it into the coffee cream. Pour into individual ramekins and refrigerate for two hours.

To Serve

Turn out of ramekin dishes and serve with whipped cream or a salad of fresh orange segments on the side.

Raspberry Semifreddo with Ginger Biscuits —

Semifreddo is an Italian term that means 'half-frozen'. And that's what it is, a semi-frozen dessert — and you don't need an ice-cream machine to make it. It's rich and creamy, and you can substitute pretty much any fruit for the raspberries (plums are splendid). Best of all, you can use jam-quality berries to make this simple frozen dessert — it makes no sense to turn expensive premium-grade fruit into ice-cream!

Ingredients / Serves 8–10

Raspberry Semifreddo

200g raspberries
2 tbsp icing sugar
1 tbsp water
9 egg whites
400g sugar
zest of 1 lemon
670ml cream, whipped to soft peaks
ginger biscuits to serve
100g raspberries to serve

Ginger Biscuits
Makes 15–20 biscuits

100g self-raising flour
pinch of salt
1 tsp ground ginger
½ tsp ground cinnamon
2 tbsp sugar
50g unsalted butter
3 tbsp golden syrup

Method

To make the semifreddo, line a loaf tin with plastic wrap, leaving it hanging over the sides. In a food processor, blend the raspberries, icing sugar and water. Strain the purée into a bowl. Beat the egg whites until they form stiff peaks. Add the sugar and resume whisking for about three to four minutes until the mixture again forms stiff peaks. In another bowl, carefully fold the raspberry sauce and lemon zest into the whipped cream. Fold the cream into the egg whites with a metal spoon. Pour the mixture into the tin, fold the plastic wrap over to cover and freeze overnight.

To make the ginger biscuits, preheat the oven to 180°C. Grease and flour a baking sheet. Sift the dry ingredients together and add the sugar. Melt the butter, add the golden syrup and combine with the dry ingredients to form a smooth dough.

Place tablespoonfuls or walnut-sized pieces of dough on the baking sheet about five centimetres apart and flatten slightly. Bake for 12–15 minutes until they are golden brown with crisp edges. The centres should be slightly soft. Remove the tray from the oven and transfer biscuits to a wire cooling rack. Store in an airtight container. They will keep for one week in a cool dark place.

To Serve

Turn out the semifreddo, roll into a scoop or cut into slices and serve with ginger biscuits and a bowl of raspberries.

Poached Peach with Lemon Verbena Sabayon —

This exquisitely simple dessert requires little effort but produces wonderful results if you get it right — the peach skins add a soft pink hue to the syrup and the sabayon is light and delicious. The key to a great sabayon is to have the water no warmer than body temperature during cooking.

Lemon verbena is one of the greatest summer herbs, adding top-note fragrances to salads, soups, grilled fish and fruit-based desserts. It also makes the most refreshing tea. If you haven't got lemon verbena, use mint instead.

Ingredients / Serves 6

1 x 750ml bottle riesling
1 cup water
1 cup sugar
zest of 1 lemon
1 vanilla pod
6 peaches
4 egg yolks
4 tbsp sugar
2 tbsp chopped lemon verbena

Method

In a large saucepan bring 670mls of the wine, water, sugar, lemon zest and vanilla pod to the boil. Reduce the heat and simmer for two minutes. Score the top of the peaches with the tip of a sharp knife and carefully place them in the pan to poach for three minutes. Using a slotted spoon, remove them to a plate. Allow to cool enough to handle them, then remove the skins.

Reduce the poaching syrup until thick, for about five minutes. Pour about five centimetres of water into the bottom of a saucepan and bring it to a bare simmer. Whisk together the yolks, sugar and reserved riesling in a mixing bowl over the water.

Cook, whisking constantly until the mixture is a thick, pale yellow. This should take about eight minutes. Add the lemon verbena.

To Serve

Place the peaches on individual serving plates, spoon the reduced syrup around them and top with the sabayon.

Grilled Peaches with Almond Biscuit, Crème Fraîche and Mint —

I love a fresh, fragile but perfectly ripe white peach, bursting with juice. I don't think I've met anyone who doesn't, although I have come across people who don't believe they should be cooked.

Necatrines may be substituted for peaches in this classic Italian dish. I prefer to use yellow-fleshed peaches, and you can substitute almond macaroons or Italian amaretti biscuits for the almond biscuits. Occasionally, I splash a little rum over the fruit just before baking.

Ingredients / Serves 4

Almond biscuits
Makes 40

360g blanched almonds, toasted and ground

300g sugar

10g flour

4 egg whites

300g sugar

2 tsp almond essence

2 tsp lemon zest

Grilled Peaches

150g crumbled almond biscuits or store-bought amaretti

1 egg

2 tbsp light muscovado sugar / soft brown sugar

4 peaches, halved and destoned

crème fraîche for serving

mint leaves for serving

Method

To make the almond biscuits, preheat the oven to 130°C. Grease and flour a flat baking sheet or line it with non-stick baking paper. Combine the almonds, the first measure of sugar and flour. Whisk the egg whites until they form stiff peaks. Slowly add the second measure of sugar and continue to mix until glossy and stiff. Fold in the almond essence and the lemon zest and place teaspoon-sized dollops of meringue onto the prepared tray, allowing room for them to spread a little. Bake for one hour. Turn the heat off and allow the biscuits to cool in the oven for a further hour.

Remove the tray from the oven and transfer the biscuits to a wire cooling rack. Store in an airtight container. They will keep for one week.

To prepare the peaches, preheat the oven to 180°C. Combine the crumbled almond biscuits with the egg and sugar. Place spoonfuls of the mixture into the hollow in the peach where the stone has been removed. Place the peach halves in a lightly buttered ovenproof dish and bake for 30 minutes until the fruit is tender and the almond mixture has caramelised slightly.

To Serve
The peaches can be served either hot or cold with crème fraîche and snipped mint leaves.

White Chocolate Mousse and Raspberries —

This mousse is unusual because it has no cream in it. It is as light as a cloud, disappearing on the tongue, but leaving the taste of the chocolate behind.

Ingredients / Serves 6

180g white chocolate buttons

4 tbsp milk

1 egg yolk

4 egg whites

60g caster sugar

optional: mint leaves to garnish

optional: 1 cup raspberries to serve

Method

Melt the chocolate with the milk in a bowl placed over a saucepan of barely simmering water. Do not allow the bottom of the bowl to touch the water. When the chocolate has melted, add the egg yolk and mix until glossy. Whisk the egg whites and sugar until they form stiff peaks. Fold the whites into the chocolate one-third at a time. Pour into a container and refrigerate, preferably overnight.

To Serve

Serve with a sprig of mint or a pile of raspberries.

Chocolate Terrine with Mandarin Sauce —

My daughter loves chocolate, and not just any variety. Her favourite is Valrhona, the exceptionally cocoa-butter-rich chocolate from France. She grabs a small handful of this dark chocolate as she races through the restaurant kitchen after school. I pity any future boyfriends who turn up at our door hoping to impress her with a box of Roses chocolates. It just won't work.

What she loves best about great chocolate is that a little bit goes a long way. I strongly recommend searching for the best dark chocolate you can buy. Avoid anything labelled 'cooking chocolate'. Really good dark chocolate has intense aromatic notes of dried fruits, tea and berry fruits.

The use of olive oil in this sweet sauce is unusual, but it gives a pleasant texture and enhances the citrus fragrance. This sauce is also fabulous poured over ice-cream.

Ingredients

Chocolate Terrine

250g unsalted butter

250g caster sugar

250g best-quality dark chocolate, chopped

5 eggs

1 tbsp flour

Mandarin Sauce
Makes approximately 2 cups

3 medium mandarins

100ml water

100g sugar

100ml lemon-infused olive oil

Method

To make the terrine, heat the oven to 180°C. Cut the butter into pieces and place it in a deep bowl. Pour the sugar over the butter and then place the chocolate on top. (This process ensures that the butter and sugar dissolve and create a lining on the bowl so that the chocolate won't stick to it.) Melt the chocolate mixture over a pot of barely simmering water, then remove it from the heat. Transfer the mixture to an electric mixer with a whisk attachment. In a separate bowl, whisk the eggs and flour. With the mixer machine running, pour this egg mixture onto the chocolate and continue to whisk until it becomes smooth and shiny.

Line a terrine or loaf tin with greaseproof paper and pour the chocolate mixture into it. Cover with foil and place the dish in a deep roasting dish. Add enough water to the roasting dish to come halfway up the sides of the terrine then place it in the oven for 1½ hours. Remove the terrine from the oven and cool before refrigerating it overnight to set.

To make the sauce, first remove the bitterness from the mandarin peel by placing the whole unpeeled mandarins into a pot, covering them with cold water. Bring the water to the boil then drain the mandarins, discarding the water. Return the mandarins to the pot and repeat the process. Do this a total of five times. In a separate pot bring the 100ml water and sugar to a boil, reduce the heat and cook for two minutes. Remove from the heat and allow the syrup to cool. Put the mandarins and the sugar syrup into a liquidiser and purée until smooth. Slowly pour in the oil and blend. In the refrigerator this sauce will keep indefinitely.

To Serve

Cut the terrine into one-centimetre thick slices. (You will not want much more than this because it is so rich. Remember, you can always go back for more.) Place each slice on individual serving plates and serve the mandarin sauce alongside each piece and top with a spoonful of softly whipped cream. I like to sprinkle some chopped nuts over mine, but this could be seen as gilding the lily.

**Chocolate Terrine with
Mandarin Sauce**
Recipe on page 213

Chocolate Mousse —

Rich yet subtle, this is the easiest chocolate mousse recipe ever, with the whipped egg whites making it wonderfully light. It is also a great base recipe. While the chocolate is melting with the milk, it can be infused with orange peel, cardamom or cinnamon.

Invest in some martini-shaped cocktail glasses to serve the mousse in, or pour the finished mousse into egg cups or ramekins.

Ingredients / Serves 6

180g dark chocolate

80ml milk

1 egg yolk

4 egg whites

60g sugar

Method

Melt the chocolate with the milk in a bowl placed over a pot of barely simmering water. Do not allow the bottom of the bowl to come into contact with the water. Add the egg yolk and stir until the mixture becomes glossy. In a separate bowl, whisk the egg whites with the sugar until stiff peaks form. Fold the whites into the chocolate mix one-third at a time, mixing until it is all just incorporated. Pour into a container and refrigerate (preferably overnight). The colour will change from pale beige to a much deeper shade.

To Serve

Divide the mousse evenly into martini glasses and top with vanilla-flavoured whipped cream, bananas, raspberries or chopped nuts.

Rich Rice Pudding, Poached Tamarillos and Marmalade —

This is possibly a special-occasion dish, as it requires spending a bit of time at the stove, but it is well worth the effort.

Ingredients / Serves 6

Rice Pudding

½ cup short-grain rice

3 cups milk

1 vanilla bean

1 tbsp grated orange zest

2 tbsp grated lemon zest

½ tsp salt

100g sugar

2 egg yolks

50g unsalted butter

125g quality marmalade to serve

Poached Tamarillos

8 tamarillos, peeled

750ml water

250g sugar

2 cinnamon quills

6 cloves

Method

To make the rice pudding, bring a pot of water to a vigorous boil. Add the rice and cook for two minutes, then drain, discarding the water. Heat the milk to a medium temperature in a deep saucepan. Add the vanilla bean and citrus zest. Add the rice and salt. Cover the pan with a tight-fitting lid and cook for 50 minutes. Remove the lid and stir the rice until any remaining milk has evaporated. Stir in the sugar and yolks. Keep stirring until the rice has thickened slightly. Add the butter and stir until it melts.

To poach the tamarillos, first score a cross in the base of the fruit and then immerse them for a few seconds in boiling water. The skin will peel off easily. Bring the water, sugar and spices to the boil. Lower the heat, add the tamarillos and cook for five minutes until just tender. Remove the tamarillos and set aside, reserving the syrup. Allow the tamarillos to cool, then slice them into quarters. Whisk a little of the syrup into the marmalade to loosen it slightly.

To Serve

Divide the rice between six bowls. Place the sliced, poached tamarillos on the side and drizzle the thinned marmalade over the top of the puddings.

Pear and Almond Frangipane Tart —

The frangipane cream can be made several days in advance if you wish, as it needs to be chilled before using. The pears can be replaced with apples or quinces. Brush the tart with some melted apricot jam as it comes out of the oven if you wish.

Ingredients / Serves 8

Poached Pears

180g sugar

550ml water

1 vanilla bean

6 Beurre Bosc pears, peeled, cored and quartered

Tart

120g unsalted butter

150g sugar

200g ground almonds

optional: 1 tsp orange blossom water

2 eggs

1x 23-cm baked sweet shortcrust pastry shell, store-bought

poached pewars

icing sugar to dust

Method

To poach the pears, bring the sugar, water and vanilla bean to a gentle boil in a saucepan. Add the pears and reduce the heat to low. Cover with a piece of greaseproof paper and cook for 15 minutes or until the pears are tender. Remove the pears from the syrup, drain and chill. Carefully slice the quarters.

To make the tart, preheat the oven to 180°C. To bake the pastry see lemon tart recipe on page 228, but use a tart tin, not a springform pan. Cream the butter and sugar until pale and fluffy, preferably in a mixer rather than a food processor as you want to get in as much air as possible. Add the almonds, orange blossom water (if using) and eggs and mix well. Pour the batter into the baked pastry shell. Arrange the pear slices attractively in circles, each slice overlapping the next, and push them gently into the almond batter. Cook the tart for 30 minutes or until golden brown. Remove from the oven and set aside to cool until required.

To Serve

Dust the tart with icing sugar and serve it warm with ice-cream or softly whipped cream.

Fine Apple Tart —

Individual tarts are so elegant, and there is something special about having a whole one to yourself. They are easy to make, and can be prepared well ahead and either served cold or reheated in the oven. You have to avoid a lot of double entendres when writing an introduction for a tart, no matter how elegant it may be.

Ingredients / Makes 4 tarts

200g store-bought puff pastry

8 Granny Smith or Golden Delicious apples, peeled, cored and cut in half lengthways

juice of ½ a lemon

3 tbsp caster sugar

75g unsalted butter, cut into pieces

Method

Preheat the oven to 180°C. Roll the pastry out thinly and cut out four circles, using an 18-centimetre plate as a guide. Pierce the pastry with a fork and lay the circles out on greaseproof paper on a flat baking sheet. Cover with greaseproof paper and refrigerate. Thinly slice the apple and sprinkle with the lemon juice to prevent discoloration. Take the baking sheet from the refrigerator and place the apple slices in concentric circles around the pastries, leaving a five-millimetre gap around the outside edges to allow the pastry to rise and form a border. Sprinkle the apples with the sugar and dot the butter evenly over each tart. Bake the tarts for 20 minutes until the apples are lightly coloured and the pastry has puffed up around the edges.

To Serve

Drizzle with cream of add a scoop of ice-cream.

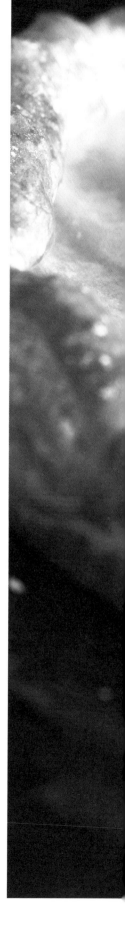

Tarte Tatin —

On my list of top 10 favourite desserts, tarte Tatin is number three, just below crème brûlée. Although the thought hadn't occurred to me till now, it's funny that they both include caramel. Anyway, I believe that there is no better hot apple dessert.

I've been cooking this tart for years and, although it's no longer on the restaurant's menu, hardly a winter goes by without someone requesting it.

So, what is tarte Tatin? The recipe requires apples to be slowly caramelised in butter and sugar, then topped with buttery puff pastry. After being finished in the oven, the tart is carefully inverted onto a plate. As the recipe involves hot caramel, care needs to be taken with this step. You need to get the caramel just right, too, or the flavours will be unpleasant.

The many stories surrounding the creation of this dessert all originate in the nineteenth century with the Tatin sisters. As legend has it, one sister was in the Hotel Tatin kitchen, just outside Paris, caramelising apples for a tart. Then the stories diverge: one suggests that she was overworked, another that she was flirting with a hunter. Regardless of the reason, the caramel and apples ended up overcooked. In an effort to rescue the dessert, she placed some pastry on top of the apples and put the pan into the oven. She later served the upside-down tart to an appreciative restaurant, and a culinary legend was born.

Always use firm dessert apples such as Granny Smith or Golden Delicious, otherwise the result will be a soft apple purée and soggy pastry.

Ingredients / Serves 2

150g store-bought puff pastry

3 tbsp caster sugar

75g unsalted butter

4 Granny Smith or Golden Delicious apples, peeled, quartered, core removed and each quarter cut into three

Method

Preheat the oven to 180°C. You will need a 20-centimetre ovenproof omelette pan with deep sides that will allow the caramel to bubble and the pastry to rise. Roll the pastry out to a thickness of three millimetres then use the pan as a guide to cut a circle slightly larger than the base of the pan. Put the pastry on a plate, cover it with greaseproof paper and refrigerate until required. Place the pan on a low heat and sprinkle the sugar over the bottom. Add the butter in small pieces and melt, swirling the butter and sugar together until they begin to caramelise lightly and turn a delicate amber colour.

Arrange the apples in a circle around the pan. Increase the heat slightly so that the apple juices mix with the caramel. Swirl the pan occasionally to prevent the apples from sticking. When the caramel becomes a rich golden colour, place the pastry over the top of the apples and put the pan into the oven. Cook for 12 minutes until the pastry rises. Remove the tart from the oven and place it back over a low heat to loosen any apples that may have stuck.

Invert a plate over the top of the pan and carefully flip the pan and plate over, taking great care not to get any caramel on your hands.

To Serve

Pour all the apple caramel juices over the tart and serve with crème fraîche, vanilla ice-cream or whipped cream flavoured with vanilla.

Deep Lemon Tart with Raspberries and Citrus Syrup —

Every cook should have a decent lemon tart recipe and this is mine. It's remarkably simple, resulting in a mouth-puckering dessert that is seductively elegant. The tart uses ludicrous quantities of eggs, cream and sugar, but it's not as if you eat this every night. If you wish to make a shallow tart — and I really don't know why you would — halve the recipe.

Ingredients / Serves 8

Tart

2 egg whites, whisked lightly together
18 eggs
700g sugar
juice of 10 lemons, strained
600ml cream
400g store-bought sweet short-crust pastry
1 punnet raspberries

Citrus Syrup
Makes 2 cups

1 cup sugar
1 cup lemon juice
1 cup orange juice

Method

Juice the lemons and strain the juice. Break the eggs into a bowl with the sugar and whisk lightly until smooth and blended. Gently whisk in the lemon juice. Whisk the cream until lightly thickened and carefully combine with the egg mixture. Refrigerate this mix, ideally for 12 hours, or while the pastry cooks.

Preheat the oven to 160°C. Line a deep 23-centimetre loose-bottomed springform pan with the pastry, ensuring that it overhangs the top edge. Do not trim it off. Line the pastry with a decent-sized piece of greaseproof paper and fill it with rice or baking beans. Bake the pastry blind until a light golden-brown — about 45 minutes — and remove from the oven. Lift out the greaseproof paper and beans and set aside. Brush the insides of the pastry with the beaten egg white, patching up any holes with leftover pastry, and return the case to the oven for 10 minutes. This will seal the pastry and stop it from becoming soggy. Remove the case from the oven and cool. Once cool, trim the top of the pastry in line with the top of the baking tin by gently running a serrated knife around it.

Give the mixture a gentle stir before pouring the filling into the pastry case, then bake for one to 1¹/₂ hours. Remove the tart from the oven and allow it to cool on the kitchen bench.

To make the syrup, combine the ingredients in a heavy-based saucepan and bring to a simmer. Continue to cook until it reduces to a heavy syrup, then remove from the heat and cool in the refrigerator. Do not stir the syrup after it has cooled.

To Serve
Pile raspberries on top of the tart and drizzle with half a cup of citrus syrup.

Mascarpone Cream with Berry Salad —

This recipe is like making your own fresh sweet cheese. Although it is based on the French recipe coeur à la crème, which uses heart-shaped, perforated ceramic moulds lined with wet muslin to allow the whey to drain away, I simply let the cheese drain in a damp muslin bag. Then spoon it out and serve it with fresh berries.

Ingredients / Serves 6

Mascarpone Cream

150g mascarpone	
100g cream cheese	
125g caster sugar	
1 cup cream	
½ cup thick plain yoghurt	

Berry Salad

150g blackberries or boysenberries	
150g raspberries	
150g strawberries	
3 basil leaves	
3 tbsp sugar	
3 tbsp water	

Method

To make the mascarpone cream, blend the mascarpone, cream cheese and sugar until smooth. Add the cream and yoghurt and blend briefly.

Cut a big piece of muslin and soak it in cold water and wring it out. Line a large strainer with the muslin and suspend it over a clean bowl. Spoon in the cheese. Tie the ends of the muslin to form a bag, suspend it from a wooden spoon over the bowl and refrigerate overnight.

To make the berry salad, put all the ingredients into a saucepan. Bring to the boil and remove from the heat. Transfer to a bowl to cool.

To Serve

Unmould the cheese and serve with berry salad spooned over the top.

Strawberry Sponge with Lemon Verbena and Orange Salad —

This is not a Victoria sponge at all, but as its texture is exactly like a real sponge I have not come up with an alternative name for it. This soft, pretty dessert is like eating strawberry air.

Ingredients / Serves 6

Strawberry Juice

1 cup sugar

2 cups water

1 punnet strawberries, hulled and rinsed

Strawbery Sponge

2 punnets strawberries

½ cup strawberry juice or more to taste

½ tsp powdered gelatine per 100ml liquid

Lemon Verbena and Orange Salad

4 oranges, segments removed

4 lemon verbena leaves

Method

To make the strawberry juice bring the sugar and water to the boil for two minutes in a saucepan. Chop the strawberries and put them into a deep bowl. Pour the hot syrup over the strawberries and allow to cool. There will be enough heat in the syrup to cook them. Once the syrup has cooled, pour the syrup and strawberries through a sieve, crushing the strawberries as you do. Discard the solids left in the sieve, rinse it, and repeat the process. The juice can be stored in the refrigerator for two weeks.

To make the sponge, purée the strawberries in a food processor until smooth, then pass the purée through a sieve. Mix the remaining pulp with the pre-made strawberry juice. Use enough juice to obtain a strong strawberry flavour. You should ideally end up with about 500ml. Pour the purée into a measuring jug and allow ½ a teaspoon of gelatine for every 100ml. Dissolve the gelatine in a little hot water and stir it into the purée. Pour the mixture into an electric mixer with a whisk attachment and whip it on high speed — this will take some time, but the syrup will gradually increase in volume to form a light, airy sponge and the colour will change to a soft pink. Pour the sponge into a deep 15-centimetre container and refrigerate for about four hours until set. Remove the sponge from the mould and cut it into rectangles.

To make the salad, cut the tops and bottoms off the oranges, and remove the peel and white pith. Hold each orange over a bowl to catch the juice, and cut between the membranes of the segments, carefully lifting them out. Add the segments to the bowl with the juices. Finely slice the verbena leaves and toss through the oranges.

To Serve

Carefully place pieces of the sponge on individual serving plates. Place a small mound of salad next to each sponge. Drizzle with extra strawberry juice if you have any left over.

Strawberry and Orange Salad, Mascarpone Puff Pastry and Candied Capsicums —

Sometimes you just have to go beyond a bowl of strawberries dredged in icing sugar with whipped cream and another store-bought pavlova. Maybe you need to impress guests or maybe you just want to learn some new kitchen moves on a rainy day. Either way, this dessert makes the most of summer fruit, combining them as interesting partners in traditional preparations. Frankly, store-bought pavlovas will become a distant memory.

The idea for this dish is originally from American chef David Burke. I have always enjoyed using vegetables in desserts. Candied tomatoes are sensational, as is young fennel. Candying even makes my most detested vegetable palatable. And, no, I will not tell you what it is. This is a very summery dessert, and once you have candied the capsicums, the rest is incredibly simple. The capsicums may also be used served with ice-cream or fruit-based cakes.

Ingredients / Serves 4

4 sheets store-bought puff pastry

200g mascarpone cheese

zest and juice of 1 lime

4 oranges

2 punnets strawberries, hulled, washed
and sliced

4 tbsp candied capsicums

icing sugar to dust

Candied Capsicums

2 red capsicums, finely chopped

2 yellow capsicums, finely chopped

1 cup sugar

1 cup cider or apple juice

juice of 1 orange

2 tbsp brandy

Method

Preheat the oven to 180°C. Cut the
pastry sheets into rectangular shapes
10cm x 5cm. They seem large but
do shrink. Place the pastry onto a
greased baking tray. Place a piece of
greaseproof paper over the top of the
pastry and cover with another flat
baking tray. Bake in the oven until
golden, then remove the top baking
tray and continue to cook for a further
five minutes. Remove the pastries to a
cooling rack away from draughts. Mix
the mascarpone with the lime zest and
juice and refrigerate.

Cut the tops and bottoms off
the oranges, and use a sharp knife
to remove the peel and white pith
from the segments. Hold each orange
over a bowl to catch the juice, and
cut between the membranes of the
segments, carefully lifting them out.

To make the candied capsicums,
combine the capsicums, sugar and
cider or apple juice in a heavy-based
saucepan and heat gently until the
mixture begins to caramelise. Do not
stir the contents of the pot, otherwise
they will crystallise. Remove from the
heat and whisk in the orange juice and
brandy. Transfer to a jar and store at
room temperature. They will keep for
three months.

To Serve

Horizontally slice each puff pastry
rectangle into three pieces. Place a slice
in the centre of a plate and spread with
mascarpone. Top with a layer of sliced
strawberries, and place the middle
layer of pastry on top. Spread with
more mascarpone and carefully place
the orange segments along the slice.
Finally, place the last piece of pastry
on top of the oranges and spoon the
candied capsicums over the top. Dust
with icing sugar.

Strawberry and Orange Salad,
**Mascarpone Puff Pastry and
Candied Capsicums**
Recipe on page 235

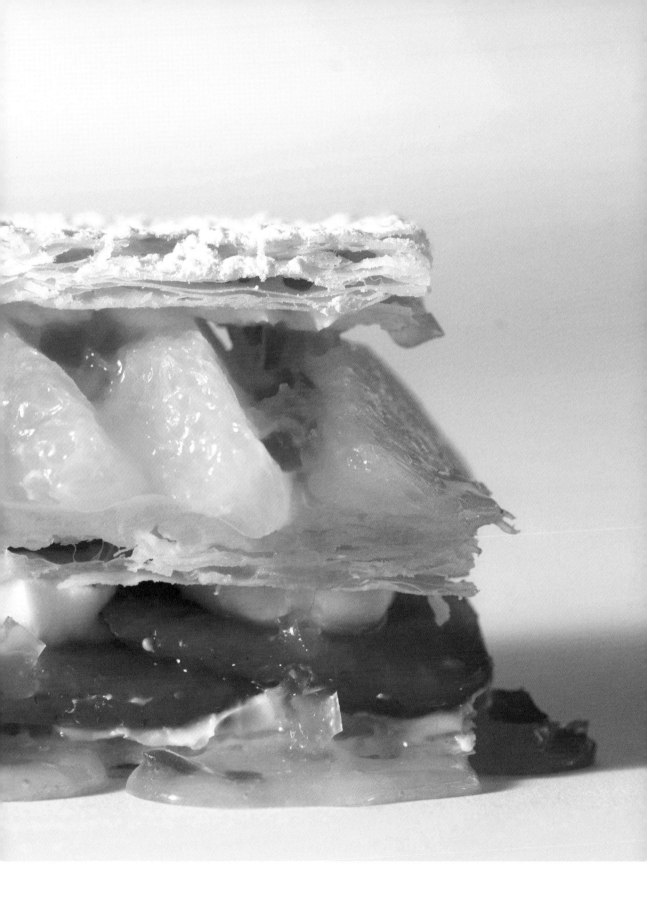

Christmas Pudding —

At Christmas time the restaurant is so busy with events, lunches and dinners that I pretty much say goodbye to my long-suffering family, knowing that I won't see them again until Christmas Eve. Unfortunately, that is sometimes the life of a restaurant family.

On Christmas Day, with three sets of family to see, I end up eating brunch with one, then moving on to my mother's for a roast turkey lunch at which she insists on lighting candles, despite the fact that we are eating at midday. I am always seduced by the sentimental feelings that candles evoke, making life seem better and family squabbles irrelevant. Dinner is more candles and yet another roast turkey, the skin of the turkey crisp and golden in the candlelight, and even more sentiment.

I contribute Christmas puddings for both the turkey feasts and that's about the extent of my involvement, apart from rescuing the gravy. Everyone insists that I don't cook, which is a blessing, but I wonder what I would cook if my mother and mother-in-law let me.

Apart from the pudding, I would begin with the Italian-inspired tomato and bread salad on page 63. It's simple, light and easy to make, and hints at the promise of summer. My main course would be a roast shoulder of lamb, rubbed with olive oil, lemon juice, garlic and rosemary.

Ingredients /
Makes 4 small puddings

1 cup raisins

150g sultanas

150g currants

100g almonds, blanched and chopped

180g Shreddo suet

juice and zest of 1 orange

juice and zest of 1 lemon

1 Granny Smith apple, unpeeled, cored and grated

1 medium carrot, peeled and grated

120g flour

180g raw sugar

3 eggs

pinch of salt

pinch of ground cinnamon

½ tsp mixed spice

60g mixed peel

120ml brandy

150ml stout beer

Method

Combine all the ingredients and mix thoroughly. Cover and refrigerate for 48 hours. Preheat the oven to 150°C. Grease four 12-centimetre pudding basins and divide the mixture between them. Press the mixture down firmly to make sure that it is compact. Wipe the basin rims with a damp cloth to remove any spills. Cut four circles of greaseproof paper big enough to fit the top of the basins. Lightly grease the circles then place one on top of each pudding, pressing firmly to form a seal.

Lay a large circle of damp muslin over each basin, stretch it taut and use string to tie it around the rim. Line a deep baking dish with some greaseproof paper and place the puddings on top of the paper. Put the dish into the oven, adding enough water to come halfway up the sides of the puddings. Cover the entire baking dish with foil. Cut a small hole in the centre of the foil to allow a small amount of steam to escape. Close the oven door and bake for eight hours.

Remove the basins from the oven and let them cool before removing the muslin. Wash the muslin in clean water and allow it to dry. Leave the greaseproof paper in place and wipe the edges of the basins clean before stretching the washed muslin back over the puddings. Tie them tightly and seal by brushing the muslin with a little melted butter. If using the puddings as gifts, cover with foil before wrapping them up.

To Serve

Custard, whipped cream and berries are perfect companions for the pudding.

Cherry Financier —

At home we keep a bowl of cherries on the kitchen bench throughout the season. Everybody grabs two or three of the irresistibly glossy, crimson clusters as they pass and discreetly discards the pips directly into the garden. But some occasions call for something a little more elaborate, and sometimes even cherries must be cooked.

Financiers are usually baked as individual cakes and take their name from their resemblance to gold bars. These extremely addictive little cakes are also known as friands. A truly great financier has a good crust, so the oven must be hot. You can use blueberries, raspberries or blackberries if you prefer and, as this recipe suggests, make it in a large tray to be sliced later

Ingredients / Serves 8

200g unsalted butter
250g icing sugar
4 tbsp flour
70g ground almonds
½ tsp baking powder
salt
4 egg whites
zest of 1 lemon
½ cup pitted cherries

Method

Preheat the oven to 200°C. Grease a 20-centimetre by 15-centimetre baking tin and and line it with non-stick baking paper. Melt the butter in a saucepan until it turns a nut-brown colour, then tip it into a stainless steel bowl and refrigerate to cool. The butter must remain liquid.

Sift together the dry ingredients and combine in a mixing bowl with the egg whites. Blend until thoroughly mixed. Slowly add the melted butter and the lemon zest.

Pour the batter into the prepared tin and spread the cherries over the top. Bake for 25 minutes or until a light brown crust forms on top and the financier is springy to the touch. Remove from the oven and transfer to a wire cooling rack.

To Serve

Cut into fingers, dust with icing sugar and serve with whipped cream or yoghurt. Best eaten on the day they're made.

Plum, Walnut Oil and Sweet Wine Cake with Plum Compote —

When thinking of making a plum version of upside-down pineapple cake, I suddenly remembered the golden and tender-crumbed olive oil and sauterne cake made famous by chef Alice Waters. I substituted walnut oil because I felt it would better suit the plums, and used a local dessert wine instead of sauterne. It worked.

Ingredients / Serves 6–8

Plum Compote

1½ cups water

½ cup sugar

500g black Doris or Purple King plums, halved and destoned

juice of 1 lemon

Cake

5 eggs, separated

¾ cup sugar

1 tbsp orange zest

100ml walnut oil

125ml dessert wine

1 cup flour

pinch of salt

2 egg whites

½ tsp cream of tartar

6 plums, halved, pitted and quartered

plain yoghurt to serve

ground cinnamon for dusting

Method

First, make the compote by bringing the water and sugar to a simmer. Add the plum halves, bring back to the boil and cook until tender — about 10 minutes. Add the lemon juice, then pour into a bowl and allow to cool.

To make the cake, preheat the oven to 180°C. Line the base of an 18-centimetre round or 20-centimetre square cake tin with baking paper. Beat the egg yolks with half the sugar until pale and creamy. Beat in the orange zest, oil and wine. Sift the flour and salt and add to the yolk mixture. Combine the egg whites and cream of tartar, and whisk until soft peaks form. Add the remaining sugar and whisk to stiff peaks. Carefully fold in the yolk mixture.

Arrange the plum quarters around the base of the lined tin. Pour in the batter and bake for 45 minutes. Turn the oven off and leave the cake for 10 minutes before transferring to a wire cooling rack.

To Serve

Cut into pieces and serve with spoonfuls of plum compote and yoghurt. Dust with a touch of ground cinnamon.

Orange and Almond Cake —

I love making this cake — everything fits into the food processor, so there's next to no washing up. Delightfully moist, it is also a pretty cake to look at, with its dark top in marked contrast to its golden-yellow interior. I serve it with mascarpone cheese and slices of fresh orange, but you could substitute yoghurt or whipped cream.

Ingredients / Serves 8–12 or makes 12–16 muffin-sized mini-cakes

3 whole oranges, peeled
9 eggs
375g sugar
375g ground almonds
2 tsp baking powder

Mascarpone Cream
Makes 1 litre

zest and juice of 2 limes
1 litre cream
1 vanilla bean
1 tsp citric acid or 1 tsp white wine vinegar

Method

Preheat the oven to 180°C and grease and line a 30-centimetre cake tin with baking paper. (It can also be made in muffin pans, as pictured.) Simmer the oranges in a large saucepan of water for two hours, changing the water three times during the process. Cool, then cut the oranges in half and remove the pips. Squeeze out any excess liquid that may have been absorbed during the cooking process. Place the orange pieces in a food processor and blend until smooth. Add the eggs and sugar and blend for three minutes. Add the almonds and baking powder and blend for two minutes. Pour into the prepared tin and bake for one hour. (If using muffin pans, bake for 45 minutes.) Remove from the oven and cool in the tin before transferring to a wire cooling rack. Store in an airtight container. This cake freezes well.

To make the marscapone cream, bring the zest, cream and vanilla bean to a rolling boil. Boil for exactly four minutes until the cream separates. Add the lime juice and citric acid or vinegar, then return to the boil. Lower the heat and simmer gently for exactly one minute, then remove from the heat. Pour the cream through a fine sieve into a stainless-steel bowl, then refrigerate until set. Rinse the vanilla bean clean under cold running water. Line a clean sieve with damp muslin and place it over a larger bowl. Pour in the set cream, cover with plastic wrap, and return to the fridge for 24 hours. Scoop the mascarpone into a clean container. It will keep in the refrigerator for seven to 10 days.

To Serve

Dust with icing sugar and serve with mascarpone cream.

Lemon Shortbread —

These delicate and fragrant shortbread biscuits make a simple dessert that was quite common on restaurant menus last century. It has fallen from favour, possibly because it's so simple, but that really is the charm of it. You can also serve the shortbread with a berry salad.

Ingredients / Makes 15–20

250g unsalted butter, softened
¾ cup caster sugar
2 cups flour
½ cup cornflour
pinch of salt
zest of 1 lemon
fresh berries for serving
mascarpone or crème fraîche to serve
optional: berry salad (see page 231) to serve

Method

Preheat the oven to 180°C. Grease and flour a baking sheet. In an electric mixer with a beater attachment, cream the butter and sugar until pale and creamy. This usually takes five to seven minutes — the longer you cream the better the shortbread.

Turn the mixer to the lowest setting and add the flour, cornflour, salt and lemon zest. Be careful not to overmix. Roll the dough into logs and refrigerate. Cut the logs into biscuit-sized slices ($\frac{1}{2}$-centimetre thick) and place on the baking sheet five centimetres apart. Bake for 10 minutes. Remove the tray from the oven and carefully transfer the biscuits to a wire cooling rack. Store in an airtight container.

To assemble the dessert, you will need two shortbreads per serving. Place a biscuit on each plate and put a teaspoon of crème fraîche or marscapone in the centre. Arrange a circle of berries around the perimeter. Top with another biscuit and dust with icing sugar.

To Serve

Serve with a berry salad if desired.

Butters & Sauces.

'Butter! Give me butter, always butter!' exclaimed famous French chef Fernand Point. Even though I use butter in moderation, I have occasionally been accused of a certain degree of butter-lust, and was once proclaimed the King of Fat. While olive oil has its place, there's something about butter that makes food taste better. Fish pan-fried in nut-brown butter and finished with a squeeze of lemon juice and a little vinegar tastes much better than if cooked in olive oil.

Flavoured butters add a new dimension to grilled meats, and butter whisked with a little water and tossed over cooked green vegetables will make them more satisfying. Properly creamed butter and sugar will aerate cakes, while in pastry it melts away, leaving a delightfully flaky texture. I use unsalted butter in my kitchen, so when I need to spread it on bread I whisk the butter in a mixer until fluffy and pale, then sprinkle it with flakes of sea salt.

This Section

Mustard and Chive Butter	**256**
Chimichurri Butter	**256**
Thyme Butter	**257**
Anchovy Butter	**257**
Chive Aïoli	**258**
Hollandaise Sauce	**259**
Salsa Creosa	**262**
Jam Jar Viniagrette	**262**
Salsa Verde	**263**
Sauce Vierge	**263**

Mustard and Chive Butter —

This butter's terrific on grilled meat or fish and will keep in the freezer for months.

Ingredients

200g unsalted butter

2 tbsp grain mustard

1 tbsp lemon zest

3 tbsp chopped chives

salt and freshly ground black pepper

Method

Soften the butter and add the mustard and lemon zest. Mix with a wooden spoon until smooth. Add the chives and season to taste with the salt and pepper. Spread the butter onto a sheet of greaseproof paper and roll into a log. It will keep in the refrigerator for four weeks.

Chimichurri Butter —

This Argentinean recipe is delicious with grilled meats or cooked green vegetables. Simply dollop on a teaspoonful just before serving so it gently melts into your food.

Ingredients

1 cup chopped parsley

1 tsp chopped oregano

2 tsp chopped garlic

freshly ground black pepper

100g unsalted butter, softened

1 tbsp white wine vinegar

salt

Method

Place the herbs, garlic and pepper into a food processor and with the machine running add the butter. Add the vinegar and season with salt. Whiz again. Spread the butter onto a sheet of greaseproof paper and roll into a log. It will keep in the refrigerator for four weeks.

Thyme Butter —

Herb butters provide terrific fragrant highlights, and thyme butter is particularly useful with seafood.

Ingredients

1 bunch parsley, chopped

4 tbsp chopped thyme

2 tsp chopped garlic

freshly ground black pepper

100g unsalted butter, softened

1 tbsp white wine vinegar

½ teaspoon salt

Method

To make the thyme butter, place the herbs, garlic and pepper in a food processor and with the machine running add the butter. Then add the vinegar and salt. Spread the butter onto a sheet of greaseproof paper and roll into a log. Refrigerate until ready to use. It will keep in the refrigerator for four weeks and will keep for months in the freezer.

Anchovy Butter —

People are scared of using anchovies, for no real reason that I can understand other than maybe they are using cheap and inferior brands. Quality anchovies provide savoury notes, and this butter can be used over grilled or barbecued meats, with seafood, on roasted vegetables or cooked green vegetables to give them a dynamic lift.

Ingredients

300g unsalted butter, softened

5 anchovies

juice of 1 lemon

freshly ground black pepper

Method

Place the butter, anchovies and lemon juice in a food processor and process until smooth and season with pepper. Spread the butter onto a sheet of greaseproof paper and roll into a log. Refrigerate until ready to use. It will keep in the refrigerator for four weeks and will keep for months in the freezer.

Chive Aïoli —

Just grilling some salmon? This is the perfect accompaniment.

Ingredients

90g baked potato pulp or mashed potato, sieved

3 cloves garlic, crushed

2 hard-boiled egg yolks

1 egg yolk, raw

juice of 1 lemon

1 cup olive oil

4 tbsp chopped chives

salt

Method

Combine the potato pulp, garlic, cooked and raw egg yolks and lemon juice in a bowl and stir with a wooden spoon until smooth. (Do not use a food processor.) Slowly beat in the oil — it should end up quite thick. Add the chives, then season with salt to taste. It will keep in the refrigerator for 10 days.

Hollandaise Sauce —

This recipe uses standard butter rather than the usual clarified kind that most recipes call for. Clarified butter makes an oily and sometimes rancid-tasting sauce, whereas standard butter improves the texture and flavour but also prevents the sauce from breaking up. Although many cooks suggest using white pepper to avoid having a black speckled sauce, I still prefer to use black. Traditionally, hollandaise is made with lemon juice only, but the addition of vinegar gives it a lift.

Ingredients

200g unsalted butter, at room temperature

75ml white wine vinegar

50ml water

3 egg yolks

juice of ½ lemon

salt and freshly ground black pepper

Method

Cut the butter into tablespoon-sized chunks. In a small saucepan, reduce the vinegar and water to one tablespoon. Transfer this reduction into a bowl with sloping sides that will sit easily on a pot of barely simmering water. Make sure the water does not touch the base of the bowl or you may end up scrambling the eggs. Add the egg yolks to the bowl and whisk until thick. Add the butter gradually, whisking continuously until the sauce is thick and creamy. If the sauce becomes too thick, add a tablespoon of hot water. Season with the lemon juice, salt and pepper.

Variations

Béarnaise

Use tarragon vinegar instead of wine vinegar and add freshly chopped tarragon to the finished sauce. This is the classic partner to grilled fillet steak.

Mousseline

Fold 75ml of whipped cream through the finished hollandaise. It is fabulous served over cold poached salmon.

Paloise

Add two tablespoons of chopped mint. Enjoy this with roast lamb.

Maltaise

Replace the lemon juice with blood orange juice, or normal orange juice will suffice. This is perfect with asparagus.

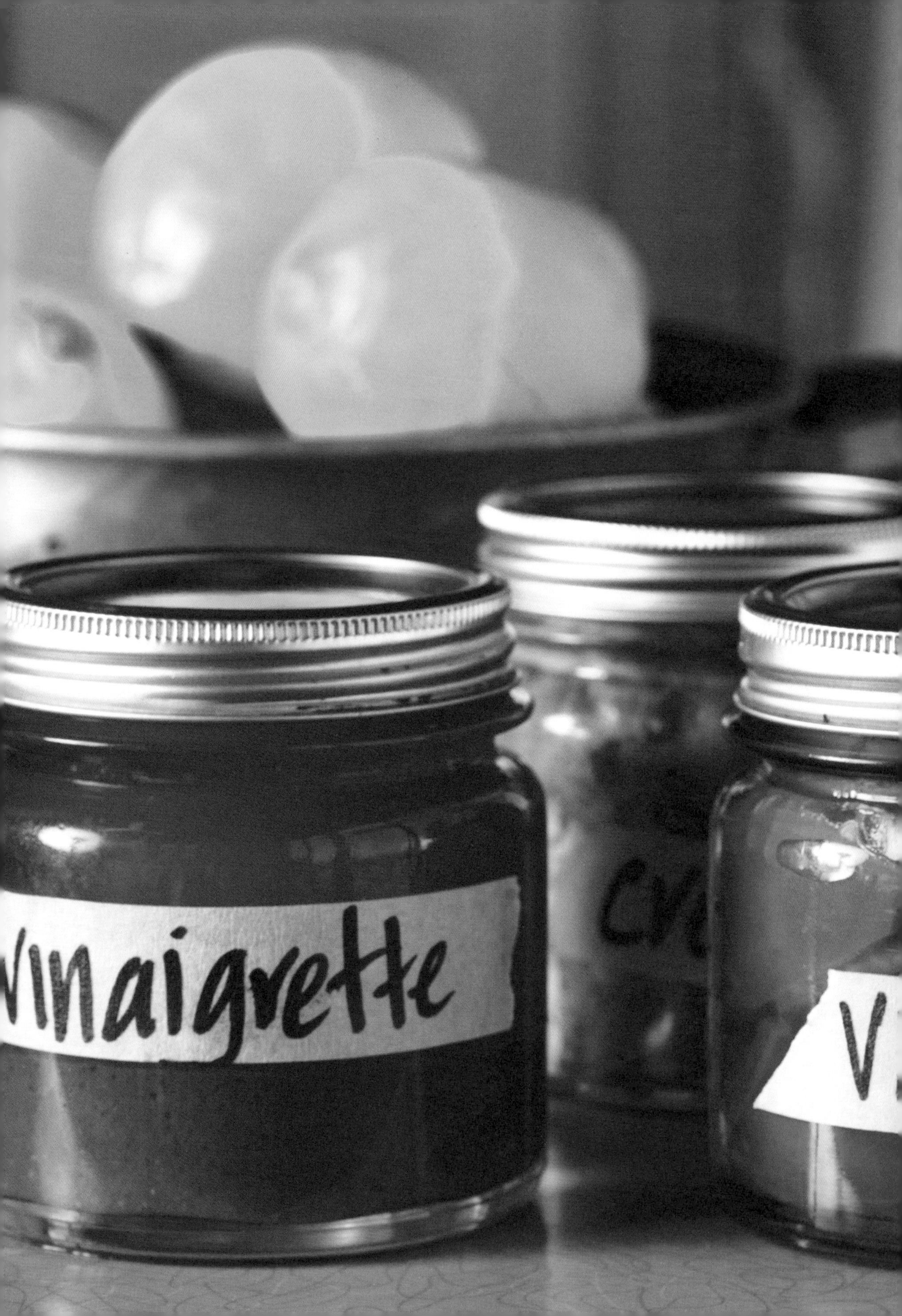
vinaigrette

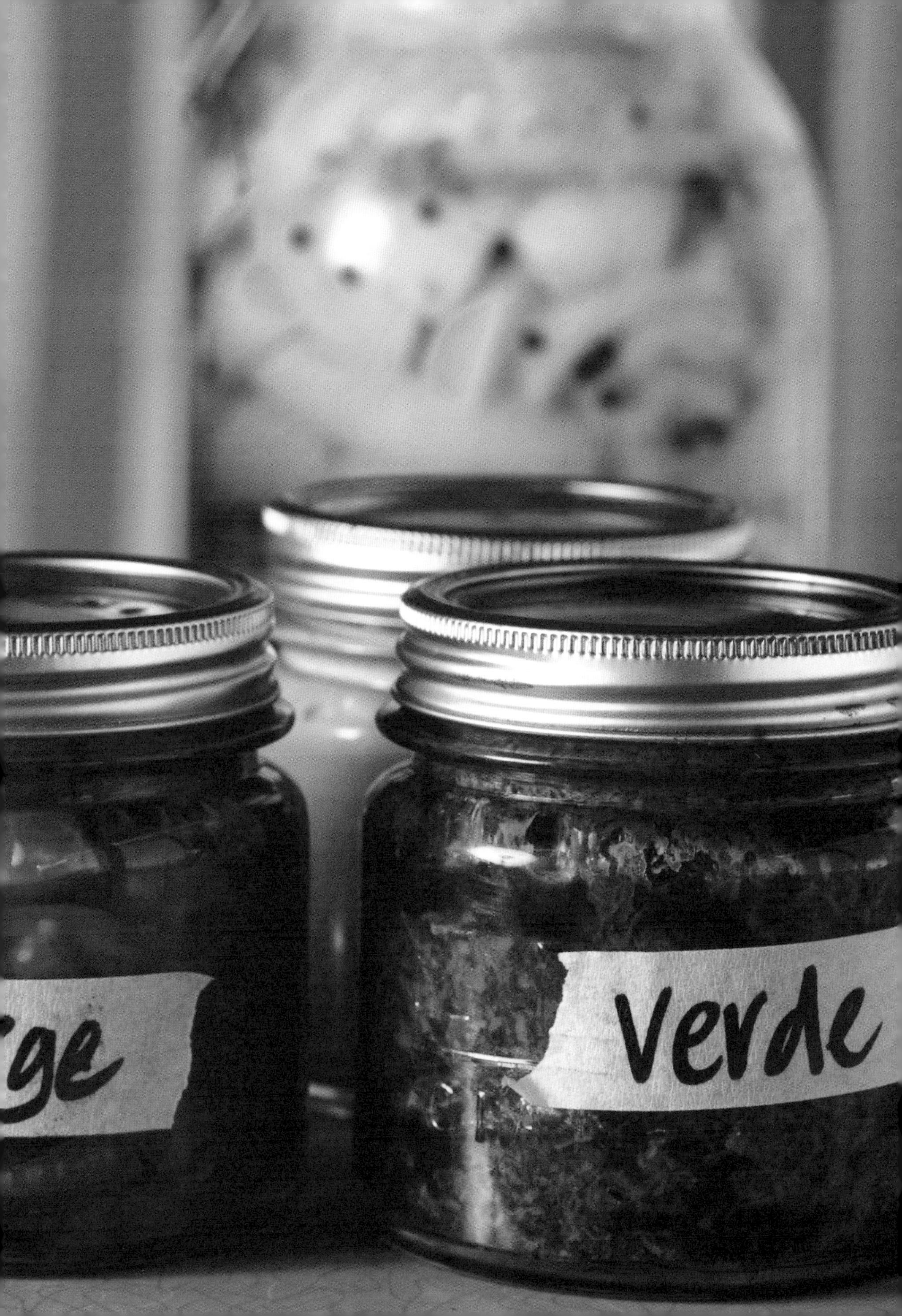
ge
verde

Salsa Creosa —

Friends introduced me to this magnificent salsa. The recipe comes from *Cuisine of the Sun,* by the great French chef Roger Vergé. It must be made at least 24 hours ahead.

Ingredients

1 telegraph cucumber, peeled

3 tomatoes

1 onion, finely chopped

1 red or yellow capsicum, finely chopped

100g gherkins, finely chopped

100g capers, rinsed and chopped

1 tsp chopped French tarragon

200ml olive oil

3 tbsp red wine vinegar

4 tbsp Dijon mustard

salt and freshly ground black pepper

Method

Cut the cucumber in half lengthways and remove the seeds by dragging a teaspoon from one end to the other. Cut the tomatoes in half and squeeze out the seeds and juice. Cut all the vegetables into small cubes, preferably no bigger than a pea. Pile the vegetables into a bowl and mix in the gherkins, capers, tarragon, oil, vinegar and mustard. Season with salt and pepper. Pour into a jar and refrigerate. It will keep in the refrigerator for two months.

Jam Jar Viniagrette —

I always have a jar of this on hand.

Ingredients

60ml red wine vinegar

2 tsp Dijon mustard

2 cloves garlic, finely chopped

salt to taste

180ml extra virgin olive oil

Method

Shake the ingredients together in a glass jar with a secure lid. Strain and discard any solids. Return the vinaigrette to the jar and refrigerate. It will keep in the refrigerator for four weeks.

Salsa Verde —

This Italian sauce has the ability to awaken and stimulate the tastebuds. I keep a jar in the fridge as it is perfect for a tapas-style platter.

Ingredients

1 bunch parsley, approx 170g

1 bunch basil, approx 50g

6 anchovies

2 tbsp capers

2 cloves garlic, finely chopped

1 small red onion, chopped

3 tbsp white wine vinegar

3 tbsp olive oil

salt and freshly ground black pepper

Method

Place the herbs, anchovies, capers, garlic, onion and wine vinegar in a food processor and blend until smooth. You will need to scrape down the sides occasionally. When smooth, add the oil in a thin stream and season carefully with salt and pepper. Pour into a jar and refrigerate. It will keep in the refrigerator for four weeks.

Sauce Vierge —

Quite literally 'virgin sauce', for this recipe the quality of the tomatoes is paramount — they must be ripe and full of flavour. Delicately flavoured and aromatic, it is fabulous with thinly sliced raw fish, or spooned over cooked fillets of fish.

Ingredients

10 coriander seeds, toasted

400ml extra virgin olive oil

juice of 1 orange, 1 grapefruit and 1 lemon

2 tomatoes, seeded and chopped

4 basil leaves, chopped

Method

Infuse the seeds in the oil for 30 minutes. Strain and discard the seeds. Whisk the juices and oil and add to the tomato and basil. Pour into a jar and refrigerate. It will keep in the refrigerator for one week.

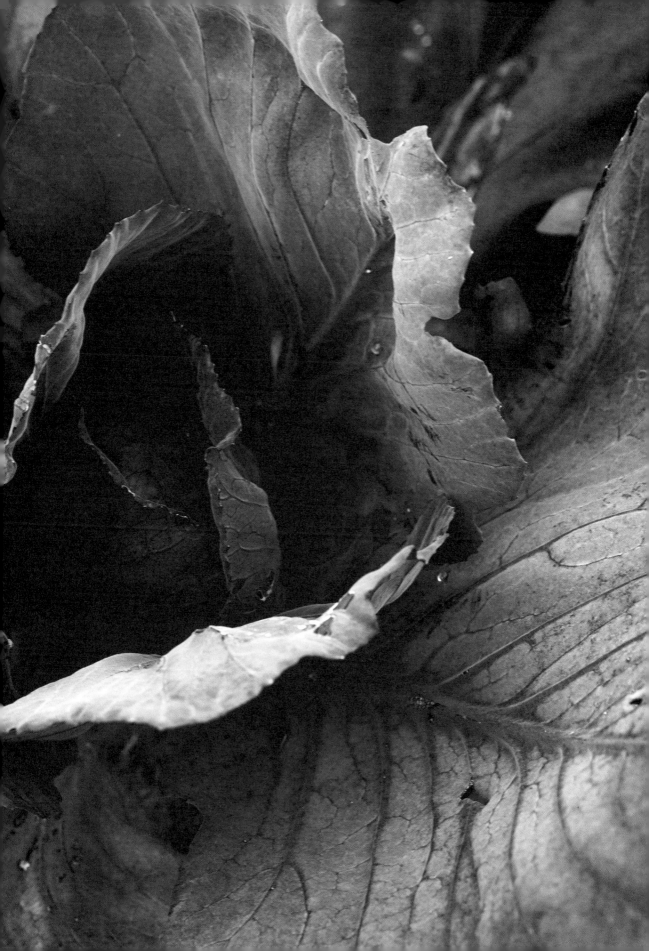

Drinks.

At the restaurant we like to give our guests a complimentary drink, usually served in a shot glass, when they are first seated. It's another way of saying 'welcome', but we also like to think of it as a small reward for the day's work, and for you finally making it to lunch or dinner. The snowball has a sense of frivolity about it.

A great Bloody Mary can be a drink of pure beauty under the right circumstances (and I have recently read of an American restaurant that has an entire Bloody Mary menu, such is the popularity of the drink there). It's not always alcohol based — we might use lemon syrup as a base for a more soothing or refreshing drink.

Use any of these recipes as your own small incentive to get on with things. It's like saying 'well done, I deserve this' to yourself.

This Section

Lemon Syrup — **270**

Ginger Spider — **271**

Bloody Mary — **272**

Snowball — **272**

Hot Chocolate — **273**

Lemon Syrup —

Our lemon trees produce fruit twice a year — in November and December, and again in April and May. We make syrup whenever we have ripe fruit, and we raid the lemon trees at my sister's house when she is not there, although I think she suspects something ...

Ingredients / Makes 2 litres

zest and juice of 6 lemons

1.3kg sugar

50g tartaric acid

25g citric acid

1 tbsp Epsom salts

8 cups boiling water

Method

Grate the rinds of the lemons — I use a microplane grater — and squeeze out the juice. Mix the rind and juice with the sugar, tartaric acid, citric acid and Epsom salts. Add the boiling water and stir until the sugar dissolves. Pour the syrup into jars or bottles and store in a cool place.

To Serve

When you're thirsty, pour some of the syrup into a jug and fill with lots of crushed ice and still or sparkling water. Alternatively, add a generous splash to a gin and tonic. It's also super when drizzled neat over vanilla ice-cream.

Ginger Spider —

When we had Marty's restaurant at Waikanae Beach, one of the top-selling drinks was the Ginger Spider — it was actually designed for children, but more popular with adults. Ian, our head chef, came up with this simple variation on the old-fashioned ice-cream and soda drink, the Spider. It's usually made with lemonade or Coca-Cola, but we made ours with ginger beer. Being purists, we originally tried to make our own ginger beer using fresh ginger, sugar, yeast and lemon. It was a disaster, with bottles exploding all over our storeroom. To make a really good Ginger Spider, choose a ginger beer that is not too sweet and not a carbonated soft drink. Eventually, we came across the thirst-quenching nectar that is Rebecca Hardie-Boys's Ginger Beer.

Ingredients / Makes 1 drink

vanilla ice-cream

ginger beer

Adult version

vodka

ginger beer

lime juice

Method

In a large glass wider at the top than the bottom, place a scoop of vanilla ice-cream and then add the ginger beer. Stir until it's creamy, then top with another scoop of ice-cream.

For the adult version, dump the ice-cream, pour a shot of vodka over some ice with a squeeze of lime, top with ginger beer and you have a Moscow Mule — also thirst-quenching.

Bloody Mary —

If ever I'm asked about the perfect drink pairing for cheese on toast, I'll say a Bloody Mary. Not that I expect anyone to care enough to want to know, although some might suggest that I have a drinking problem for even contemplating such a match.

The drink is believed to have been invented in 1921 by Fernand Petiot, the barman at Harry's New York Bar in Paris.

My secret addition is horseradish sauce, which adds an indefinable piquancy. Make sure you always use top-quality vodka. And never imbibe a Bloody Mary before midday — everyone will know you are hungover. Make sure the tomato juice and vodka are cold — it will make ice unnecessary.

Ingredients / Makes 1 drink

juice of half a lemon

1 tsp horseradish sauce

2 drops Tabasco sauce

50ml vodka

100ml tomato juice

celery salt and freshly ground black pepper

Method

Squeeze the lemon juice into a tall glass. Add the horseradish and Tabasco sauces, mixing to a wet paste. Pour over the vodka and tomato juice. Stir well and season.

Snowball —

The yellow colour of the Snowball cocktail has always intrigued me, as has the advocaat used in the drink. I have never found another use for this rich liqueur, so it sits around in a dark cupboard waiting to come out once a year — a bit like Christmas, really.

Until the age of eight, I lived in the dreary north of England — Cheshire, which was too close to Manchester for me. Most of my memories are of a drab and miserable place, but I remember my parents' Christmas Eve parties with fondness. They usually involved dancing — with Herb Alpert, Brazil '66 and Sergio Mendes, and Henry Mancini on the record player — and glasses of frothy Snowballs. I think the first time my sister got drunk was at the age of five when she sat behind an armchair drinking one of these golden light-hearted cocktails. Similar in taste to an eggnog, a Snowball is spectacularly simple to make.

Ingredients / Makes 1 drink

60ml advocaat

squeeze of lime juice

lemonade

Method

Put the advocaat into a glass, add a squeeze of lime juice and top up with the lemonade, stirring carefully. If you stir too hard you'll quickly find out how the drink got its name!

Hot Chocolate —

I am not much of a tea drinker so something I love to drink instead is hot chocolate. It must be decadently indulgent, rich and luxurious, made with real, unadulterated dark chocolate and not with drinking chocolate, which is usually made from pressed cocoa powder so it has no cocoa butter left in it. The chocolate must be melted into the milk as it heats to create that all-important velvety texture. It can be infused with cardamom, cloves, orange peel or even chilli. It's truly just like being wrapped in a thermal blanket on a chilly winter's day.

Ingredients / Serves 4

500ml milk

2 tbsp sugar

2 tbsp water

140g good-quality dark chocolate, coarsely chopped

Method
Place the milk in a heavy-bottomed saucepan. Dissolve the sugar in the water and add to the milk. Place the pot over a medium heat. Add the chocolate and whisk until the milk has

heated through but is not boiling and the chocolate has melted. Remove the mixture from the heat. If you have a stick blender, use it to froth the milk. This will give it an outrageously seductive texture and prevent a skin forming.

To Serve
Serve in small cups, preferably with a teaspoon of whipped cream.

Liquid Assets.

I once went to a small dinner party where all the wines were served without any of the guests being able to read the labels. This is not unusual at Wine and Food Society or Beefsteak and Burgundy Club dinners, and having hosted many such events over the years, I am usually comfortable in such environments. This particular dinner turned out to be on another level altogether. All the wines were French, and the small number of dinner guests was knowledgeable enough to be accurately guessing vintages and naming vineyards that I had never heard of. I watched one guest literally chew his wine across his palate with his mouth wide open. When I discreetly tried to do the same, the wine poured inelegantly from my mouth. Guests were describing chemical compounds present in the wine that I had no idea existed. I did not know that there is a flavour in pinot noir best described as lipstick — I still don't know if that's a good thing or not. I left the dinner that night slightly intimidated and trembling with fear, my confidence shaken.

The next morning I reviewed the evening in my mind and came to the conclusion that fortunately not everyone drinks and analyses wine in that way — including many winemakers I have met — and that true connoisseurs of wine can terrify the rest of us. As the inimitable Peter Rumble once said to me, 'If you think a wine tastes just like your grandmother's old socks, then that's what it tastes like and don't be afraid of saying so.'

I believe that wine and food matching is a subjective matter. I personally adore champagne, particularly rosé, and most dishes go with champagne so I am in luck, if not out of pocket. I never look for perfect matching, though, and I generally choose what it is I wish to drink first. The main point is that the relationship between wine and food is important, and together they provide a common bond between people.

This Section

Pinot Gris	**280**
Riesling	**280**
Sauvignon Blanc	**280**
Chardonnay	**281**
Viognier	**281**
Tempranillo	**281**
Bordeaux-style	**282**
Dessert Wines	**282**
Sherry	**282**
Calvados	**282**

Pinot Gris —

Until a couple of years ago, there were two types of white wine drinkers in New Zealand: chardonnay and sauvignon blanc. In the wings, waiting quietly and patiently to be discovered as a delicious and refreshing food wine, was riesling.

Instead, along came the juggernaut that is pinot gris. Not as overpowering as chardonnay or as acidic as sauvignon blanc, it's almost certainly a crowd-pleaser of a wine.

Although a New Zealand style has yet to be defined, there are two very different styles of this species of *Vitis vinifera*. For a start, the colours range from pale to deep gold, with shades of pink and copper.

The French style — pinot gris — has peach-like sweetness, richness and weight, all cream and custard, with floral bouquets of spices, apples, pears and melons and a slight sweetness on the palate.

The Italian style — pinot grigio — tends to be fresh, crisp and austere, light-bodied and delicate. There is a good argument to start labelling New Zealand wines accordingly, as this would enable consumers to understand the difference between the styles.

Riesling —

Most non-riesling drinkers are confused about this magnificent grape, assuming that it is a cheap, sweet wine. This could not be further from the truth.

Winemakers, chefs and other insiders know that rieslings are the most captivating and thrilling wines in the world, and we are always justifying to a wider audience why we drink them. Rieslings are often found in wine lists tucked discreetly under 'chardonnay' and 'pinot noir' or disguised as either 'varietals' or 'aromatics', bundled up with viognier and pinot gris.

Rieslings have distinct floral and apple aromas, often combined with flinty mineral elements. Expect subtle notes of rose petals, pears and stonefruit — and the smell of kerosene is actually considered a positive. So, whether they're delicate and complex or bone dry and crisp, once you have started drinking riesling you'll find it irresistible. Don't forget the intensely flavoured botrytis or late-picked wines.

Because of the balance between acid and sweet, rieslings are great with buttery fish dishes, spicy sausages and most Asian cuisines. Their unmistakable thirst-quenching quality makes them a perfect pairing with salty or spicy foods.

Sauvignon Blanc —

Few grape varieties show the pure expression of the grape, the soil and temperature, or the terroir in which they are grown like sauvignon blanc does. Cool climates emphasise the herbaceous qualities while warm climates bring out the more melon and citrusy flavours. We produce arguably the finest sauvignon blancs in the world, with bold, fresh and lively flavours. Light, crisp and grassy, they are fabulous to drink with salads, tomato dishes and most seafood, chicken and egg dishes. Occasionally the wines are briefly aged in oak to soften the wine and to enhance the smokiness the grape can display, but mostly they are fermented in stainless steel to maintain the intensity of the flavours. The French call it sancerre or pouilly fume, and when it is allowed to develop noble rot on the vines and blended with semillon, it produces the greatest dessert wines in the world.

Chardonnay —

I stopped drinking New Zealand chardonnay years ago when it became unfriendly to food, was overpowered with oak, and I ended up with a splitting headache the next day. (Though that may have been due to how much chardonnay I had drunk.)

In recent years, though, the oak has diminished and more emphasis has been placed on malo-lactic fermentation to soften the acidity; the malic acid providing sour apple characters and the lactic acid providing buttery flavours. Therefore, in the mysterious world of wine and food matching — and trust me, there are no real rules — a buttery recipe calls for chardonnay, and I prefer to drink those with a little oak to bring out the smoky, vanilla, caramel flavours of the grape, and those that are generally more opulent. Chardonnay without any oak tends to be softer, fruitier and more austere; these styles are suited to less buttery dishes.

Viognier —

I am often tempted to match raw fish with sake, the alcoholic beverage obtained by the multiple fermentation of rice and often incorrectly called rice wine. However, the rich flavours can clash with raw fish.

Because I'm not really a beer drinker unless I have just mowed the lawns, I felt unqualified to recommend beer, so instead I thought about the sixth flavour present in raw seafood — umami.

Umami cancels tannins in wines, allowing fruit, mineral and floral elements to shine, leaving the door wide open for wine matching. Even pinot noir is excellent with raw fish, but my first choice is viognier.

The creamy yet clean taste of viognier makes a wide variety of flavours acceptable. It is golden in colour, with a sweet nose but a dry, soft and delicate finish.

Viogniers are wonderfully fragrant wines, with hints of orange blossoms, roses, candied lemon peel, apricots and peaches.

Tempranillo —

When out for dinner recently, I was poured a tempranillo with the main course — a tagine of fresh tuna. My hosts had planned to serve burgundy, but after tasting the food, decided that the two did not go together.

I've often overlooked tempranillo, thinking of it as a blending grape, but I quickly discovered what excellent food wines they make.

Pronounced temp-rah-nee-yoh,

the name means early. It possibly came about because the grape ripens earlier than other varietals, but also the wine can be consumed when young. Nonetheless, it ages well. Tempranillos are complex wines, with a medley of aromas and flavours and intense deep-purple colours. From a nose containing blackberries, plums, prunes and, even, truffles, the wines have a velvety smooth taste of minerals, liquorice and leather and are almost meaty. They are perfect with stews, casseroles and aromatic dishes.

Bordeaux-style —

Generally rich and opulent, bordeaux is made from a blend of grapes, predominantly cabernet sauvignon and cabernet franc, that is further mixed with a blend of cabernet merlot for its soft yet full, lingering flavours, and syrah for its peppery and dried-herb notes.

Dessert Wines —

Contrary to popular opinion, dessert wines are not always big and sticky. They are, in fact, potent, sweet and full of flavour — the perfect end to a dinner. The grapes are picked late in the harvest to allow the residual sugars to concentrate. Occasionally, noble rot (botrytis) is allowed to develop, which concentrates the sugars as the water in the grapes evaporates.

Late harvest rieslings are probably the most popular varieties, along with chardonnays and semillons.

Hints of pineapple, coconut, apricot, honeysuckle and caramel are not unusual and discovering the many complexities of these wines is part of the fun of drinking them. Wine should be sweeter than the food it accompanies, so serve these wines with fruit and baked or creamy desserts, never chocolate.

Sherry —

Usually drunk as an aperitif before the meal, sherry can also be served as a dessert wine. It is possible to drink a chilled fino-style sherry throughout a meal — it is a fabulous match for seafood dishes. Because its structure is so similar to sake and rice wine, manzanilla sherry, which is very light and dry, is a brilliant match for sushi, sashimi and other oriental dishes. Fino and manzanilla sherries are light in colour, dry and delicate and should be served chilled.

Amontillado is more versatile, and can be served at room temperature with soups or rare-cooked game. The richer and more powerful dry oloroso, with its toasty and nutty aromas, can be served like a vintage port at the end of a meal.

Calvados —

Some of France's greatest gourmet specialities are produced in the rich, rolling countryside of Calvados. Butter and cream from Normandy are used to produce the great cheeses camembert and boursin. It is the birthplace of the egg-rich bread brioche and its scallops, mussels and oysters are held in high regard. Calvados is also home to some of Normandy's nine million apple trees, which are harvested to make Calvados brandy.

The apples are pressed and the juice is then fermented into cider, which is distilled and aged in oak for at least two years. During this process it acquires its complex apple flavours, fragrant bouquet and deep gold shades.

The longer it is aged, the smoother the taste. The most common type of Calvados is the rich and distinctive pays d'auge. Non-vintage blends are classified in a similar way to brandy — three stars indicates two years in oak, VO four years and XO or Napoleon a minimum of six years.

Served neat, on ice or with a splash of tonic water, Calvados is a great way to end a meal. It is also fantastic with apple tarts, especially if they are served with cream. If you cannot find any Calvados, go for a gewürztraminer.

Acknowledgements.

There are a number of people to thank, to whom I am deeply indebted. If I thought cooking was a hard job, writing is much harder, and I have been lucky in having the assistance of some very talented people. At the *Listener*, Pamela Stirling has been tremendous in her support and encouragement, and in giving me the freedom to write about whatever I want to.

Jane Ussher, a beautiful person and supremely talented photographer, whose rich images capture the essence of the food, because that's what we wanted it to be about, has made every fourth Monday something to look forward to.

If my words and recipes make any sense at all, it is due in no small part to Alison Mudford, my sub-editor. Even though I am a cook, much of what I do is by instinct and I was not used to thinking about food in grams, millilitres or how big a cake tin really is. That I now do is thanks to her. H and Wicky deserve thanks for suggesting that I try writing in the first place. Jenny Farrell took the first leap of faith with my writing about food, and her feedback is always inspirational and amusing. To her I owe an enormous thank you.

Special thanks to Rachel Taulelei of Yellow Brick Road for her seafood, her enthusiasm and for sharing a philosophy on food and eating.

Writing a weekly column takes an enormous amount of time, and that I am able to do so is due to the incredible team of people who work for me at the restaurant. Thanks to Stephen, Rob, Shamus, Amy, Ian and Lena in the kitchen, whose enthusiastic discussions about food, and what it means to all of us, keep me inspired, and to Angela, John-Paul and the rest of the waiting staff who genuinely care about our guests. I am extremely grateful to Edie, my office manager, who keeps me focused when she can see a wave of procrastination washing over me. At Random House, Nicola Legat saw the possibility of the book, her enthusiasm made it real, and Rebecca Lal, possibly the toughest boss I have ever had, kept me on track.

Gavin Bradley, my remarkable business partner, also a remarkable cook, but most of all a truly remarkable friend.

My family has always been a source of inspiration, love and support. The best times I have had around the dinner table have always been with them.

Index.

aïoli, chive 258
Almonds,
  orange and almond cake 247
  pear and almond frangipane tart 221
anchovy butter 257
Apples
  fine apple tart 222
  tarte tatin 227
Artichokes
  Jerusalem artichoke and apple soup 36
  baked prosciutto-wrapped globe
    artichokes and broad bean purée
    with red capsicum oil 129
  salad of Jerusalem artichoke, almonds
    and watermelon with honeyed
    olive oil dressing 68
Asparagus
  pan-roasted scallops and crispy
    potatoes with asparagus and
    anchovy butter 104
  asparagus salad with soft-boiled-egg
    dressing 52
  asparagus soup with goat's curd 34
  asparagus with prosciutto and
    parmesan 92

Beans
  fettuccine with poached oysters and
    broad beans 121
  grilled tuna with scarlet runners,
    prosciutto and potato salad with
    caper dressing 161
  miso-braised pork belly with prawns
    and white beans 124
  salad of broad beans, pecorino cheese
    and mint 54
  salad of scarlet runner beans with
    tomatoes, almonds and sweet
    onion vinaigrette 71
  scarlet runner beans with pasta and
    blue cheese cream 122
  white bean salad, young fennel and
    gruyère cheese 58
Beef
  beef à la ficelle 174
  grilled steak with rosemary and garlic
    fried potatoes, green beans and
    reduced pan juices 177
  pan-fried fillet steak with potato
    gnocchi, prosciutto and brussel
    sprouts, grain mustard sauce 178
  slow-cooked beef cheeks, smoked eel,
    young carrots and celeriac purée
    170
  the perfect steak sandwich 89
Bread
  brioche 18

fruit bread 20
Italian-style bread and tomato salad
    63
rolls, simple 23
b'stilla 151
Butter
  anchovy butter 257
  chimichurri butter 257
  mustard and chive butter 256
  thyme butter 257

Cake
  orange and almond cake 247
  plum, walnut oil and sweet wine cake
    with plum compote 244
carpaccio of zucchini, parmesan, olive oil
    and lemon juice 130
cassoulet, seafood 153
Cauliflower
  cauliflower couscous, sautéed with
    parmesan cheese 142
  cauliflower risotto 141
ceviche with pickled rock melon and pine
    nut vinaigrette 113
cherry financier 243
Chicken
  chicken, potato and hazelnut terrine
    with asparagus and sweetcorn
    salad 148
  rice congee with chicken and oysters
    144
chimichurri butter 256
Chives
  chive aïoli 258
  chive and mustard butter 256
Chocolate
  hot chocolate 273
  chocolate mousse 217
  white chocolate mousse and
    raspberries 211
  chocolate terrine with mandarin
    sauce 213
christmas pudding 240
citrus syrup 228
Cockles
  fish braised with tomatoes, mussels
    and cockles 164
  spaghetti, cockles and fresh tomato
    sugo 116
  steamed cockles, potato gnocchi,
    anchovies and olive oil 118
coffee and anise bavarois 202
crayfish, grilled with thyme butter and
    warm potato salad 106
crème brûlée, orange and cardamom 199

Desserts & Baking
  baked meringues with poached
    cherries and toffee popcorn 194
  basil panna cotta with berry coulis
    197
  cherry financier 243
  chocolate mousse 217
  chocolate terrine with mandarin
    sauce 213
  christmas pudding 238
  coffee and anise bavarois 202
  fine apple tart 222
  grilled peaches with almond biscuit,
    crème fraîche and mint 209
  lemon tart with raspberries and citrus
    syrup 228
  lemon shortbread 248
  mascarpone cream with berry salad
    231
  orange and almond cake 247
  orange and cardamom crème brûlée
    199
  pear and almond frangipane tart 221
  plum, walnut oil and sweet wine cake
    with plum compote 244
  poached peach with lemon verbena
    sabayon 206
  raspberry semifreddo with ginger
    biscuits 205
  rich rice pudding, poached tamarillos
    and marmalade 218
  strawberry and orange salad,
    mascarpone puff pastry and
    candied capsicums 236
  strawberry sponge with lemon
    verbena and orange salad 235
  tarte tatin 227
  white chocolate mousse and
    raspberries 211
Duck
  b'stilla 151
Dressings
  jam jar vinaigrette 262
  lemon mayonnaise 67
  pine nut vinaigrette 113
  red capsicum oil 129
  red wine vinegar dressing 88
  rock sugar dressing 158
  sashimi dressing 114
  sweet herb dressing 83
  sweet onion vinaigrette 72
Drinks
  bloody mary 272
  ginger spider 271
  hot chocolate 273
  lemon syrup 270
  snowball 272

Eggs
poached in red wine 95
straciatella 44
wrap of soft-boiled egg, rocket and sweet herb dressing 83
fettuccine with poached oysters and broad beans 121

Fish & Seafood
cedar-planked salmon with celeriac and apple remoulade 110
ceviche with pickled rock melon and pine nut vinaigrette 113
citrus-cured salmon, radish, fennel and cucumber salad 61
double-baked mussel soufflé with parsley sauce 96
double-baked whitebait soufflé 98
easy winter seafood chowder with crumbled water crackers 40
fettuccine with poached oysters and broad beans 121
grilled crayfish with thyme butter and warm potato salad 106
fish braised with tomatoes, mussels and cockles 165
grilled fish and fresh peas with prawn mashed potatoes 156
grilled fish, roast kumara purée with red wine and mushroom ragoût 162
grilled fish, smoked eel and potato salad with horseradish cream 109
grilled salmon and soba noodle salad with rock sugar dressing 158
grilled tuna with scarlet runners, prosciutto and potato salad with caper dressing 161
pan-roasted scallops and crispy potatoes with asparagus and anchovy butter 104
paua soup with fried capers 42
poached fish, with barbecued potatoes, spinach and black olive tapenade 155
raw fish with sashimi dressing and cherry tomato salad 114
rice congee with chicken and oysters 144
sautéed whitebait 103
scallop caesar salad with horseradish vinaigrette 56
seafood cassoulet 153
spaghetti, cockles and fresh tomato sugo 116
steamed cockles, potato gnocchi, anchovies and olive oil 118
whitebait fritters 100

Ginger
ginger biscuits 205
ginger spider 271
ginger syrup 64

Ham
pea and smoked ham soup with mushrooms and raisins 33
roasted sweet potato, pea and ham salad with lemon mayonnaise 67
hollandaise sauce 261

jam jar vinaigrette 262

Lamb
lamb's tongue rillette with duck liver parfait, grilled prawns and salsa verde 126
barbecued lamb rump with charred vegetables and anchovy butter 166
grilled lamb rump with chorizo sausage, chickpeas and mushroom and apple and onion salad 168

Lemons
deep lemon tart with raspberries and citrus syrup 228
lemon shortbread 248
lemon syrup 270

mascarpone cream with berry salad 231
meringues, baked with poached cherries and toffee popcorn 194
miso-braised pork belly with prawns and white beans 124

Mousse
chocolate mousse 217
white chocolate mousse and raspberries 211
mustard and chive butter 258

Oranges
orange and almond cake 247
orange and cardamom crème brûlée 199

Oysters
fettuccine with poached oysters and broad beans 121
rice congee with chicken and oysters 144

panna cotta, basil with berry coulis 197
Pasta
fettuccine with poached oysters and broad beans 121
scarlet runner beans with pasta and blue cheese cream 122
spaghetti, cockles and fresh tomato sugo 116
paua soup with fried capers 43
pea and smoked ham soup with mushroom and raisins 33

Peaches
grilled peaches with almond biscuit, crème fraîche and mint 209
poached peach with lemon verbena sabayon 206
pear and almond frangipane tart 221

Plums
plum and goat's cheese salad with ginger syrup 64
plum, walnut oil and sweet wine cake with plum compote 244

Pork
grilled pork chops with white beans, fennel and spicy sausage 187
miso-braised pork belly with prawns and white beans 124
slow-cooked pork belly with aromatic spices and plums 183
Bolognese-style pork loin braised in milk 184
barbecued pork sandwich with homemade barbecue sauce and coleslaw 87

Prosciutto
asparagus with prosciutto and parmesan 92
baked prosciutto-wrapped globe artichokes and broad bean purée with red capsicum oil 129
grilled tuna with scarlet runners, proscuitto and potato salad with caper dressing
pan-fried steak with potato gnocchi, proscuitto and brussel sprouts, grain mustard sauce 178

raspberry semifreddo with ginger biscuits 205
rice congee with chicken and oysters 144
rich rice pudding, poached tamarillos and marmalade 219

Risotto
basic 141
cauliflower 141

Salads
asparagus salad with soft-boiled-egg dressing 52
salad of broad beans, pecorino cheese and mint 54
citrus-cured salmon, radish, fennel and cucumber salad 61
Italian-style bread and tomato salad 63
plum and goat's cheese salad with ginger syrup 64
roasted sweet potato, pea and ham salad with lemon mayonnaise 67
scallop Caesar salad with horseradish vinaigrette 56
salad of scarlet runner beans with tomatoes, almonds and sweet onion vinaigrette 71
salad of Jerusalem artichoke, almonds and watermelon with honeyed olive oil dressing 68
white bean salad, young fennel and gruyère cheese 58

Salmon
cedar-planked salmon with celeriac

and apple remoulade 110
citrus-cured salmon, radish, fennel and cucumber salad 61
grilled salmon and soba noodle salad with rock sugar dressing 158

Sauces, see also syrups
barbecue sauce 87
celeriac and apple remoulade 110
chive aïoli 258
berry coulis 197
fresh tomato sugo 116
hollandaise sauce 259
mandarin sauce 213
parsley sauce 96
red wine and mushroom ragoût 162
salsa creosa 262
salsa verde 263
salsa vierge 263

Scallops
pan-roasted scallops and crispy potatoes with asparagus and anchovy butter 104
scallop Caesar salad with horseradish vinaigrette 56
scarlet runner beans with pasta and blue cheese cream 122

Soufflé
double-baked mussel soufflé with parsley sauce 96
double-baked whitebait soufflé 98

Soup
asparagus soup with goat's curd 34
bourride soup 39
easy winter seafood chowder with crumbled water crackers 40
Jerusalem artichoke and apple soup 36
paua soup with fried capers 43
pea and smoked ham soup with mushroom and raisins 33
straciatella 44
spaghetti, cockles and fresh tomato sugo 116
straciatella 44

Strawberries
strawberry and orange salad, mascarpone puff pastry and candied capsicums 236
strawberry sponge with lemon verbena and orange salad 233
sweet potato, roasted, pea and ham salad with lemon mayonnaise 67

Syrups
citrus 228
ginger 64
lemon 270

Tapenade
black olive 155
green olive 80

Tomatoes
fresh tomato sugo 116
Italian-style bread and tomato salad 63
tuna, grilled with scarlet runners, prosciutto and potato salad with caper dressing 161

Whitebait
whitebait fritters 100
sautéed whitebait 103
double-baked whitebait soufflé 98

Zucchini
carpaccio of zucchini, parmesan, olive oil and lemon juice 130

My wife Julia, my daughter Isabella and me in the kitchen at home.

Jo and Isabella whitebaiting on a river whose name we dare not speak.

I've been getting my fruit and veges from Des Yee's market garden in Waikanae for years. Des is the second generation to run his family's market garden and is still assisted by his 90-year-old mother.

Isabella and me on Waikanae beach.